Into
The Light

Other Books by Ron DelBene
with Herb Montgomery

The Breath of Life
The Hunger of the Heart
Alone with God

Into The Light

A Simple Way to Pray
with the Sick and the Dying

Ron DelBene
WITH
Mary & Herb Montgomery

The Upper Room
NASHVILLE, TENNESSEE

INTO THE LIGHT

Cover Transparency: Daniel E. Wray
Cover and Book Design: Jim Bateman
First Printing: March, 1988 (10)
*Second Printing:*March, 1989 (12)
Library of Congress Catalog Card Number: 89-051428
ISBN 0-8358-0576-X

Printed in the United States of America

To all those who have allowed me into their lives
during times of loneliness, bewilderment, and pain

and

To my friend Taylor Wingo, whose unexpected death
brought unexpected life to me.

Contents

Preface 9

1. Let There Be Light 13
2. The Breath Prayer 26
3. Sharing the Breath Prayer 41
4. Karen and Her Prayer 55
5. Journey into Death 67
6. Prayer and Healing 76
7. The Gift of Touch 84
8. The Breath Prayer Opens Other Doors 97
9. Saying Good-bye 107
10. Making the Passage to Risen Life 118
11. A Need to Tell the Story 127
12. Developing Your Own Approach 136

Preface

An icy winter wind sculpted the snowdrifts outside our home while inside Ron, Herb, and I sat warm and content in front of the fireplace. During dinner, we'd caught up on news of Ron's wife Eleanor and their two children, Paul and Anne. Now we had the rest of the evening to discuss our work and exchange ideas about future projects.

Ron had stopped over in Minneapolis while on his way back to Alabama after leading a conference out West. From time to time, he's able to arrange his travel schedule this way, and his visits are always a delight. Herb's friendship with Ron began more than twenty years ago when they were both employees of the same publishing company—Ron as a consultant in Christian education and Herb as an editor. I became friends with Ron through Herb, and the three of us (four when Eleanor is able to be there) always engage in those frank and stimulating conversations that can take place only when people feel at ease with one another and are secure in their friendship.

On this particular stopover, Ron was returning from a conference where he had addressed ways to minister to the sick and the dying. He repeated stories he'd told and spoke with enthusiasm about how effective he had found the breath prayer to be in helping people accept their illnesses and make the passage from this life to the next. At some point in the conversation I said, "You know, Ron, the work you're doing deserves a book."

This was not one of those you-really-should-write-a-book comments that are so often made and never acted upon. Ron and Herb had already coauthored three books; thus, Ron was well-acquainted with the long hours and frustrations involved in taking an idea and carrying it through to publication.

Herb and I had been writing professionally for many years, sometimes working individually but most often in collaboration. Our experience had taught us that an idea for a writing project is like a seed; once the seed is planted a germination period is required before it takes root. Although we discussed some ideas for the book that winter night, we didn't settle on a unifying theme that satisfied us. This, however, was not cause to be discouraged. The seed had been planted.

Over the next three years, the book idea came up each time we got together with Ron. We'd brainstorm a bit, but never quite got to the point of saying, "This is the way it should be written." Then in the spring of 1985, Charla Honea of The Upper Room contacted Ron. She liked his published work and, after attending one of his presentations on using the breath prayer with the sick and the dying, wanted a book on the subject. Ron, who feels more at home behind a speaker's podium than in front of a word processor, called Herb and said that it appeared the book's time had come. The two of them invited me to join as a coauthor, and I readily accepted.

Herb and I made a trip to Nashville where we met with Ron and Charla to discuss the project. Originally, we envisioned a single book that would help spiritual caregivers work with the ill and those facing death. But what about the patients themselves? Couldn't something be written especially for them? And shouldn't there be help for family and friends too? In order to meet the specific needs of everyone, we created *Into the Light* and three accompanying booklets.

When I'm Alone is for the person who is sick or dying. It includes comforting thoughts and prayers.

Near Life's End is for families and friends of someone

who is dying. It suggests what they can do to help the patient and themselves during this stress-filled time.

A Time to Mourn is for anyone who is grieving the death of a loved one.

In the months after our meeting in Nashville, manuscripts crisscrossed in the mail. Ron sent the first draft of a new chapter to us, and we returned an edited version of an earlier chapter to him.

Into the Light is now in your hands. The stories that Ron tells have touched my heart. Even after the many times I've read them in the writing and editing process, some of them still bring tears to my eyes. They are a reminder that sickness and death are part of the reality of living, but they also tell us that we who care about our brothers and sisters in Christ have a role to play. Ron shows us how, through our concern, our compassion, and our prayers, we comfort the dying and help guide them toward the light of risen life.

MARY MONTGOMERY
Minneapolis, Minnesota

Editor's Note: *The stories in this book are true. Personal names and some details have been changed to protect the privacy of the individuals involved.*

1
Let There Be Light

It was Good Friday, 1962. During spring break at the university I was attending, I had arranged to fly into my hometown in Ohio to visit a friend. Though Tom and I had been corresponding for over a year, I was writing much more frequently than he was. In our letters we talked a lot about God and religion and other interests, but in every letter there was an overriding concern: Tom Kinzer was dying.

Tom had spent many months at home. Now, because of his worsening condition, he was hospitalized again. He was in St. Joseph's, the hospital where I was born and a place I hadn't visited in several years. I remember the day of my visit as being beautifully bright. As I approached the hospital I noted that there had been a lot of changes, one of the most apparent being a new entrance. I entered the wide glass doors and went to the information desk where I asked for Tom's room number. A crisply efficient woman checked the file and said, "His wife has requested that he have no visitors. What's your name, please?"

"Ron DelBene."

"Oh, yes," she said with a nod of remembrance. "Mrs. Kinzer asked me to call when you arrived. She said she'd come down to speak to you."

I waited as the woman picked up the phone and called the room. In a few minutes—although it seemed to take much longer and I was getting a bit nervous—Louise appeared. She was a small, attractive woman whose eyes and shoulders carried an unspeakably tired look. Obviously

Tom's illness was pulling her down, too. We embraced, and she cried some as I fought my own tears, thinking I had to be strong for her sake, and after all, we were in the main reception area. Louise took my hand and led me past the information desk where she smiled wearily at the woman and said, "Thanks for calling."

While we walked down the hall, Louise explained that Tom was not up to seeing anyone. "His condition is very bad," she said, "but I know he would want you to visit."

I wondered how bad he really was, but before I could get the question out, Louise faced me and said, "Be prepared for a shock, Ron. Tom is blind now, and he can't talk. He's lost so much weight. . . . I see him every day and it's still a shock to me, but you haven't seen him since Christmas. We don't know how much longer it will be."

"Thanks for warning me," I said. "I'll be all right."

"You have no idea how much your letters meant to us," Louise said as she led the way. She stopped in front of a door leading off the main corridor. "Here we are."

We stepped into a small private room with white walls, one window, a chair, table, and bed. The blinds were drawn, the light subdued. I gasped when I looked at Tom. Pictures of concentration camp victims filled my mind, pictures of people who had wasted away. I had never been close to someone in this condition and didn't know what to say or do. I fought to catch my breath, my tears, my stomach.

Louise touched her husband's hand in a way that spoke of tenderness and love. The gesture was especially affecting because it was in such sharp contrast to the clinical starkness of the hospital room. "Tom, honey," she said, bending close to his ear, "Ron is here."

Was that a flicker of recognition on Tom's gaunt face? I thought so, but there was no more movement. I took Tom's other hand in mine. For a while I just sat there, thoughts whirling. What could I—a twenty-year-old wrapped up in theological studies—say to a thirty-four-old man who was dying and leaving behind a wife and two young children? I wanted to be comforting. I wanted to say all the right things. Of course I wanted to express myself in trendy terms professors were using that year. How heady I felt, thinking the whole world was awaiting what I had to say. As I look back, I realize how fortunate I was that these people loved me enough to listen.

I don't remember how long I talked and can recall only one very small part of what I said. But that part will be in my memory forever. Even now I can close my eyes and replay the moment: I spoke about eternal life and what it must be like to walk into the heart of God. How beautiful it must be! How radiant! How joyous! At that moment, Tom—who had not moved since we entered the room—lifted his right arm slightly off the bed. Then with thumb and index finger, he formed a circle and moved his hand twice in a slow and deliberate "okay" sign. In that instant I knew that Tom was affirming me not because my words were so convincing but because *he was actually experiencing what I was talking about.* Although he wasn't yet at the moment of death, he was making the passage to new life and discovering for himself the beauty, the radiance, the joy.

Tom's okay sign marked a holy moment for me. It was as if someone had said, "Let there be light," and the light of understanding was mine. No longer would I see death as an event but rather as a process. In the years to come, that understanding provided the foundation for my work with those moving through physical death.

I remember little of what happened after that except sharing prayer with Tom and Louise, hugging them both, and walking back down the hall. The return drive to the airport was a blur. Over and over one line kept echoing in my thoughts: *Death is not what I thought it was . . . thought it was . . . thought it was. . . .*

Two days later, just a few minutes after midnight on Easter Sunday, Tom Kinzer died. When I think of him, as I often do, it's not the body ravaged and grayed by illness that I remember. What I recall is his summoning the strength to give me the okay sign. That sign was Tom's gift to me, letting me and all with whom I share his story know that death is a passage from life as we know it into the heart of God. A passage into the light.

When Does the Dying Process Begin?

My experience with Tom was, as scripture describes it, "like a lamp shining in a dark place" (2 Pet. 1:19, TEV). Although it illuminated one area of my thinking about death, it left many shadowy corners where doubts and unanswered questions lurked. Over the years, I've confronted the doubts and tried to answer the questions in an attempt to find a way to approach death that will be helpful to the dying and meaningful for me.

We all understand that there is a moment when physical life ends—a moment when the spirit leaves the body. Through Tom Kinzer I had come to see the departure of the spirit as an event, and only part of the dying process. Now other questions rose in my thoughts, the main one being: *If dying is a process, when does the process begin?*

Years after my visit with Tom and Louise in that hospital, I was teaching at a Florida junior college and on this particular evening serving on a panel sponsored by the nursing school. The topic for discussion was death and dying. One of the other panelists was Mary Lou, a terminally ill nurse in her early thirties, who had come to share her perspective.

Mary Lou began her presentation with a clinical description of her malignancy, giving factual data about her many treatments, surgeries, and side effects. Then she shared how she was responding psychologically to the momentous shift in her life. Her presentation left us silent and near tears. When it ended, she asked for questions. These many years later, Mary Lou's responses to two of those questions stand out in my mind.

The first question was from a petite woman with silver-gray hair. "I'm also in the last stages of my physical life," she stated matter-of-factly. "The one thing I get so tired of is having people ask, 'How are you?' I know they mean well, but how do *you* handle it?"

"One day I was having a particularly hard time of it," Mary Lou replied. "I'd struggled to get out of the house and to the store to buy some groceries. A woman from my church came up to me. In the overly solicitous tone her questions always took, she asked, 'And how are you today, dear?' Looking her directly in the face, I said, 'Still dying, thank you.' "

Mary Lou laughed then, and so did the rest of us. She went on to explain that although she thought her response was a bit abrupt, it was exactly what she was feeling that day. From then on she responded to people more honestly. She believed her honesty was a learning experience for everyone. "Let's help people face their own death through ours," she said. "Then maybe they won't have as hard a time as we've had."

The other question that gave me insight was from an athletic-looking young man. "You do a lot of speaking at seminars like this," he said to Mary Lou. "Does it ever get to you that you are seen as someone who has a terminal illness?"

"The way I look at it," she began, measuring her words, "is that statistically one or two of you out of this crowd will die from some traumatic accident before I do. You see, I believe we all suffer from a terminal illness: it's called life!"

A Life View

We all suffer from a terminal illness called life. That thought opened many new areas of investigation regarding how best to help those who are sick and dying. Death is as much a fact of life as birth, but we don't usually think of our birth as beginning the dying process. In fact, while we're young and healthy, most of us give little thought to either the beginning or the ending of our life. We're just busy living it. Then something disturbing happens—sickness, accident, injury, a narrow escape, the death of a loved one—and suddenly death is very much on our mind.

As I listen to and console people during their crisis times, I often hear them say these things: "He died just the way he lived"; "She was her old self right to the very end"; "He had his house in order." When we look closely at what underlies such comments, we find a basic truth. Simply stated—barring a sudden and unexpected death—we tend to die the way we live.

What does that mean? It means that deathbed conversions are rare. Throughout our years of living, we develop a "life view" that bears directly on the way we die. Although there are as many life views as there are people, I find two broad groupings into which most of us fall. We are either self-centered (in varying degrees) or other-centered (again, in varying degrees).

Some Self-centered Qualities	Some Other-centered Qualities
Clings to money and possessions	*Shares money and possessions*
Tends to complicate	*Tends to simplify*
Neglects the spiritual self	*Enriches the spiritual self*
Lives selfishly	*Lives selflessly*

Private conversations with people who are sick and dying reveal how they have lived. Attentive listening gives clues as to how we can help individuals through the confusion, worry, and guilt so commonly experienced during the end time.

Those people who have devoted most of their energy to amassing wealth and accumulating possessions to the neglect of others seem to have a most difficult time with death. That's natural because, for them, death means the loss of everything they have valued. But for those who have shared and simplified and grown spiritually, death is one more simplification. It is a faith-filled time of letting go of all that has held them to this world and of taking that final step in their growth toward God.

A Time to Let Go—A Time to Clean Out

Ted had his own understanding of a need to let go. A laborer in his midfifties, he was a great tinkerer and saver, always the butt of jokes about his garage being full of everything except his car. Two weeks before he died, I was talking with him about letting go of things, cleaning out, preparing to move through death into another form of life. It was then that he said, "For years people have kidded me that if there's anything no one would ever want, Ted's got it! But my garage isn't the only place where I've saved things. I'm like that on the inside, too. I've saved things that I should have thrown out long ago: some grudges, some disagreements, some anger, plus a lot of things I never even looked at. I just avoided them. Maybe they're worse than the stored-up things I'm aware of."

It is commonplace for those nearing death to want to make amends and be reconciled with family and friends. But individuals need not—indeed, *must* not—wait until there is a crisis point to do that. I tell people to continually "clean out." If you have a hurt or a grudge or are angry with someone, deal with it now. Don't wait. There are so many immediate issues to confront when death is near that you don't need the added concern of unresolved conflicts from your past. If death should come suddenly, as it does for many, you have no chance to be attentive to the dying process, no opportunity to right wrongs and to die with your soul at peace.

Many of us intend to clean out and never get around to it. But some of us, rather sadly, refuse to even consider the idea because our identities come not from who we are but from what we own. The dying process then becomes a matter of tightening the grip on our possessions. An extreme example of this is a woman who stated in her will that she wanted to be buried in her expensive and prized convertible.

In contrast, I like to think of Mabel. She was a spunky woman in her eighties who lived in a small house where she had moved after her husband died some years before. Many times I find that homes of older people are crowded with possessions, but not Mabel's. Her place, though neat and cheerful, was notably sparse. One night when her death was near, I paid her a visit, and she shared how good life had been.

"You know, pastor," she said, "I never was one to hold onto things. I figured I was given them to own for a spell and then I was to pass 'em along to someone else. It's been some years now since I started giving stuff away. When birthdays or graduations or weddings come along, I look through my things and think, *What would I like so-and-so to have as a present from me?* Then I choose something and give it to that person right then and there. Why should they all wait 'til I'm dead?" With a dismissing wave of her hand, she said, "That's why there isn't much around the house anymore. And the few things that are left I've labeled as to who gets 'em."

For years, Mabel had taken pleasure in giving things away. She knew the joy that comes after the giving up, and so, too, it would be with her dying. In death, she would give her spirit up to God. That would be the ultimate simplification, the ultimate joy.

Are We Really a Resurrection People?

Speaking of Christ's victory over death, Paul asks in one of his letters: "O death, where is thy sting?" (1 Cor. 15:55). By far the majority of Christians I counsel and with whom I share the end-of-life experience would say to Paul that death still carries a mighty powerful sting. It could be likened to the sting of a deadly wasp—something to be avoided at all costs. What then does it mean for Christians to believe that Jesus died and rose, and that we therefore die and rise with him?

Our belief in an afterlife begins with baptism. Then we die and rise with Jesus into a new, grace-filled way of living. Perhaps this was more fully experienced in the past when primarily adults were baptized—and then only after a long period of intense instruction and observation by the Christian community. In the baptismal ceremony, which usually occurred on the eve of Easter, candidates stripped naked and plunged into water as a symbol of the womb of the church and their entrance into a new way of life.

Whether baptism today is done with total immersion or with water poured over the head, the reality is the same. As Christians, we proclaim that the baptized person is saved from sin and that the gates of heaven have opened. For baptized Christians, all of life is geared toward the fullness of life with God. Why is it, then, that we fear moving toward that fullness? Why has death not lost its sting for us? Possibly it is because our faith tells us one thing while our culture sends us quite a different message.

We live in a society that judges us by what it sees on the outside. The standards for beauty and wellness are defined by the media, and we come to feel that if we don't have a model's lithe figure or a trim, well-muscled physique, we literally and figuratively don't measure up. The sense of inadequacy is even worse if we are ill or handicapped. We may then feel deficient as human beings and can't believe

21

in a God whose love is so encompassing that we are loved just the way we are.

Much of our fear of death grows out of a misguided perception of God. Although scripture tells us that "God is love" (1 John 4:8, KJV), many Christians perceive God as vengeful and filled with wrath, someone who dispenses punishment, not compassion and understanding. They don't take to heart the parable of the forgiving parent and know with certainty that we are all children of God who will be welcomed home and forgiven, no matter what our sins.

When people have a negative view of God, it is little wonder they fear death. Who, after all, would want to enter into an eternal union with a harshly judgmental and punitive God? To counter such a view, our preaching and learning cannot stop at the crucifixion. We must get to the resurrection stories. In them we see the love of God manifested in Jesus who shows us that death is a passage to new life.

As Christians, we have a unique message to bring to the subject of death: *to die is not to enter into darkness but to enter into light.* Although we may not want to die and leave behind loved ones and unfinished work and the delights of this life, we have the comforting assurance that there is something more for us. Jesus' death and resurrection show us that the end of this life marks the beginning of a new one. Scripture tells us that "eye hath not seen, nor ear heard, neither have entered into the heart of man, the things which God hath prepared for them that love him" (1 Cor. 2:9, KJV). It is in light of this promise and the reality of the resurrected Lord that death loses its sting.

Prepared for Birth, Why Not for Death?

"It might be helpful if more people would talk about death and dying as an intrinsic part of life just as they do not hesitate to mention when someone is expecting a baby," wrote Dr. Elisabeth Kübler-Ross, educator on death and dying. For some time now, people have not just talked about birth but have made a real effort to help parents through the birthing process.

In 1969, Eleanor and I were the first "prepared" couple in a Minneapolis hospital to share in the delivery of our son, Paul. We completed a course in which we learned about the birthing process, how emotions and feelings are involved, and the need for the person giving birth to have a "coach" to help her through labor and delivery. My role as Eleanor's coach was to be supportive and help her focus attentively on what she was experiencing. We were told she was not to fight the contractions and the pain, and we learned practical ways of working with them.

The teaching was done by others who had already given birth. They knew we were entering into mystery and were willing to enter into that mystery with us. We were given papers outlining procedures to follow when labor pains started and assured that hospital personnel would be supportive. I remember how scared we were while at the same time excited and buoyed by the sense that this was a team effort.

In those early days of prepared childbirth, not all doctors, nurses, and hospitals were enthusiastic about the programs. Even many of our friends were uninterested in the new concept. Today the picture is quite different. Prepared childbirth is the norm. Change came about because people discovered there was another way to experience childbirth. Word spread. Things changed.

Once a baby is born, we can predict only one thing with certainty: someday that person will die. Great strides have been made to prepare for the beginning of life. But what of life's end?

Things *are* changing. We speak now of "dying with dignity," and some progress has been made in the area of prepared death. The writings and teachings of Kübler-Ross and others have contributed to our understanding of the psychological stages the dying go through. Hospital wings have been built or reconditioned to care for the terminally ill and accommodate their families. Hospices are well-established in many areas of the country. The aim of the hospice program is to enhance the quality of life for patients while helping them prepare for death. Some hospices and hospitals hold regular meetings in which patients and their families help one another by sharing experiences and problems related to their particular disease and its treatment.

If We Don't Do It, Who Will?

Although progress has been made in the area of prepared death, there is still much to be done. One area of need is in helping the dying spiritually. It is a need that we, as Christians, are best able to fill for our brothers and sisters in Christ. And I ask you, my friends, if we don't do it, who will?

It's not easy to see someone near the end of life. Reminded of our own mortality, we frequently avoid the seriously ill and the dying. Being in their presence makes us uncomfortable. Even many clergy prefer not to work with the dying because they, too, are ill at ease in such distressing circumstances.

We each have been given different gifts, and the Spirit calls us to use them in a variety of services. Not everyone is meant to work *directly* with the dying. Some serve best through their prayers, their helpfulness to the families, and thoughtful acts that let dying persons know that they have not been forgotten.

For those who feel called to work directly with the terminally ill, it is necessary to take a holistic approach. Although the person dies alone, many can be involved:

family, friends, medical personnel, church leaders, and members of the congregation. Just as it's helpful for the mother to have a coach when giving birth, the terminally ill need coaches to help them work through the dying process.

Something I've found particularly useful in working with the sick and dying is a personalized way of praying that has evolved during my own quest to be constantly and intimately in touch with God. Called the breath prayer, it can be as easily taught by lay ministers and volunteers as by ordained ministers. I invite you to learn more about this prayer so that you can use it to help the sick face their illnesses and help the dying move through the mystery of death and into the light of risen life.

2
The Breath Prayer

The call came to my office at home. "You don't know me," said a woman whose monotone suggested despondency. "I was given your name by someone who said you might help . . . my son is dying."

Such difficult words to admit. Such difficult words to hear.

"What can I do for you?" I inquired in a way that I hoped would invite her confidence.

There was a pause, and the woman seemed disbelieving as she asked, "Would you *really* be willing to help?"

"Yes, if I can," I assured her. "Why don't you tell me what you have in mind."

"Well, my name is Melanie Tukker, and my son Carl has cancer. Lately he's been having experiences that scare me. I went to the chaplain at the college, and he said he didn't know anything about such things but he knew someone who did. That's how I got your name."

So it was that I arranged to meet with Mrs. Tukker's son. My friendship with Carl was about to begin.

Our first meeting took place at the community college near the high school where Carl was still able to attend some classes. He was a handsome eighteen-year-old with curly hair, a comfortable grin, and a well-muscled build. He walked with only a slight limp, so it was hard to believe that he had already lost a leg to cancer and depended on a prosthesis. Carl had been a championship wrestler and at the time of our meeting was still taking part in some matches.

We were both ill at ease as is often the case in these circumstances. Our small talk made it plain that we were uncertain as to how we would proceed. Finally I jumped in by saying, "Your mother told me you've been having some experiences she's concerned about. Do you want to share what's been happening?"

Carl eyed me as though trying to decide if I could be trusted. Then he said, "This is probably going to sound really weird."

"So? I can handle 'weird.' "

"Before I . . . ah . . . leave home for a wrestling match, I sit on the floor of my room facing a poster on the wall. It's a picture of a big wagon wheel." For a moment his eyes met mine, and he explained, "You see, I'm really into western stuff." Carl averted his gaze again and continued in a slow, deliberate voice. "Then I put my stereo headphones on and look real hard at the center of that wagon wheel. The best way I can explain it is that it leaves me feeling centered and gives me power for my matches. When I get to the match, all I have to do is close my eyes and recall how I felt while I was looking at the wheel. It makes me feel really *up*."

We sat for a while without speaking, and then I asked, "Are you continuing to focus on the wagon wheel, Carl?"

He nodded that he was, but seemed reluctant to say anything more.

"And what's happening?"

Still he hesitated, as though not sure he could trust me. "It's like there's this light."

"Is it in the middle of the wheel?"

"Yeah!" Carl shifted suddenly and looked at me with surprise.

"Is it a bright light?"

He nodded.

"And what happens when you see it?"

"Well . . . ," he began, then broke off.

"Do you feel drawn to the light," I persisted, "and sometimes even move into it?"

"Yeah!" He was obviously amazed that I would know. "That's exactly what happens!"

The hint of a smile on Carl's face told me how relieved he was that I hadn't labeled him or his experiences as crazy. His mother had told me their family was deeply religious and described her son as a young man who believed in Jesus and in prayer. Although Carl had been going through that questioning stage typical of teens, Mrs. Tukker assured me that he hadn't given up reading his Bible. Knowing that, I ventured a question I hoped would encourage him to tell the whole story. "Carl," I said, "do you see someone in the light?"

His eyes widened as though my question validated his experience. Still, he squirmed a bit in embarrassment, and I waited a moment before asking, "Who do you see, Carl?"

"W . . . well," he faltered, "I see Jesus." He stared at me then as though sure *this* admission would label him as crazy.

Instead I said, "That's beautiful! You're a lucky young man to have had that experience!"

I don't think Carl had expected to share his experience with me or anyone else. Now that he had, he seemed amazed that I wasn't taken aback and actually *knew* about what was happening to him.

Carl didn't know that the wagon wheel he had been looking at is the same basic design used by people of many religions to focus themselves for prayer and meditation. The shape, known as a mandala, is very popular in Eastern religions. Although we don't often use the word *mandala* in our Christian tradition, we do make much use of the circle as a symbol.

I found some newsprint in the room where Carl and I were meeting and sketched the wagon wheel design from his poster. Then I added small arches at the points where the spokes touched the outer circle. "You may have seen this design done in a stained-glass window at the front or back of a church," I said. "We call it a rose window. Often at the center of the design is a symbol for God. That symbol might be a triangle, a hand, an eye, or a dove."

Carl had seen such windows in churches but didn't know their designs were anything more than decoration. When I explained that the symbols in the rose windows help us focus our meditation and prayers, he began to see that his experience wasn't so out of the ordinary. "We aren't so much to look *at* the windows," I explained, "as we are to see *beyond* the design. As we become more prayerful, we're able to use the window as a focus—we look through it and into the reign of God."

We sat quietly for a moment and Carl seemed much more at ease, so I asked, "When you're drawn into the light and see Jesus, are you able yet to walk and talk with him?"

"Well . . . sort of," he admitted with reluctance. "Sometimes it's like I'm here and there at the same time. My mom was concerned about that, which I guess is why she called you."

"What's been happening to you seems strange only because we never talk about things like this," I said. "But your experiences aren't all that uncommon, Carl. Like others who've had similar experiences, you've been given a gift from God." Carl's look told me a bridge of understanding and trust had been built between us. We talked a little more, and when the time seemed right, I asked, "How do you feel about having cancer and losing your leg?"

"It's like a bad dream," he said quietly. "I find myself wondering if maybe I'll wake up and my leg will be back on my body. Sometimes it actually feels like it's there only I can't see it."

"Have the doctors talked to you about phantom pain?"

"Yeah."

"So what's the hardest part?"

He stared at some distant point and blinked away the tears that moistened his eyes. "Not being a champion wrestler anymore is tough," he said through tense lips. "I didn't want that to end . . . sometimes having this disease just gets to be too much and I want it all to be over."

We sat without speaking, and I felt that we had said as much as we could that day. We would have more meetings, but in the meantime I wanted to leave Carl with something—something that would help him feel God's presence not just when he looked at the wheel but all the time. "Carl, before I leave, I'd like to share something with you that I've found helpful and so have a lot of other people. It's a simple little thing known as the breath prayer. Tell me, what do you usually call God? Do you say Father? Creator? Jesus? Shepherd . . . ?"

"Just 'Lord,' I guess."

"Fine. If the Lord were standing in front of you right now and asking, 'Carl, what do you want?'—what would you say?"

He closed his eyes for a time.

I repeated, "If the Lord were standing in front of you right now and asking, 'Carl, what do you want?' what would you say?"

His eyes blinked open, and without hesitation he said, "Lead me to the light."

"Okay, now let's put that together with what you normally call God and make a little prayer out of it."

Carl picked up on the idea immediately. "Lord, lead me to the light," he said, then turned the words around and seemed more satisfied with, "Lead me to the light, O Lord!"

"That seems like a very good prayer for you," I said. "Let it become your friend and use it whenever possible. You'll especially want to use it when you sit in front of your poster and feel drawn into the light."

I then wrote Carl's prayer on two index cards, gave him one and put the other in my pocket. "This will help you remember your prayer. You might want to put the card on your dresser at home or tape it to the mirror. And write LMTTLOL on your notebook as a reminder to use the prayer at school. No one else needs to know what it means. For now, it's a reminder of a prayer that only you and I share."

"Do I have to say it out loud?"

"When you're alone, you can if you like," I told him. "Or just let it come into your thoughts from time to time. I think you'll find it very comforting."

We parted then, but my thoughts stayed with Carl. I had formed a bond with an eighteen-year-old who, though he was still able to attend classes, was growing weaker as a wrestler and moving steadily toward the end of his earthly life. I resolved that for whatever time Carl had left, I would do whatever I could to guide and support him on his journey.

A Different Way to Pray

You may have noticed how, in working with Carl, I presented the idea of the breath prayer in a casual, almost offhand manner. That is because people who are seriously ill don't usually want to be *taught* anything, yet they yearn for some simple, concrete way in which to help themselves. Of course they can pray in their traditional prayer forms, but in times of great distress these often aren't enough. People feel frustrated and want something more. Frequently they tell me, "I pray, but my prayers don't seem to be going anywhere. I don't feel that God hears me."

This is not the time to respond, "Of course God hears you!" and cite scripture to prove it. Our role as spiritual caregivers is to comfort, not to convince. One of the most comforting things we can do is to acknowledge people's true feelings and give what help we can *at the moment*. We offer that immediate aid and comfort when we introduce them to a form of prayer that helps them become more aware of God's presence. This form of prayer takes its name from the Hebrew word *ruach,* which can be translated "wind," "breath," or "spirit." The *ruach* of God is breathed into all living beings. Because this way of praying reminds us that we share God's breath and comes as easily and naturally as breathing, it is known as the breath prayer.

How can prayer—any prayer—bring order and a measure of comfort out of the chaos that often accompanies sickness and terminal illness? To pray is to raise the mind and heart to God, to reach out to a God who promises, "I am with you always" (Matt. 28:20). The promise for those who are ill is this: they will never be alone with their anxiety or fear or suffering. Through it all, God will be with them. And through prayer, they are most likely to feel God's caring, comforting presence.

The breath prayer is especially effective for the dying and those who are seriously ill because it can be said so effortlessly. This simple, personal prayer arises from the heart and becomes as natural as breathing. For the sick as well as the healthy, using the breath prayer follows the apostle Paul's admonishment to "pray without ceasing" (1 Thess. 5:17, KJV). In his letter to the Romans Paul says, "Be patient in tribulation, be constant in prayer" (Rom. 12:12). Likewise in his letter to the Ephesians he tells us: "Pray at all times in the Spirit, with all prayer and supplication" (Eph. 6:18). And in yet another letter we are reminded to "continue steadfastly in prayer" (Col. 4:2). Just as breathing supports life and renews our physical body, unceasing prayer keeps us focused on God and renews our spirit.

Although the breath prayer is individualized and personal, it can also be shared. Indeed some of its effectiveness with the sick and dying lies in the sharing. When we use the breath prayer of others, we put on our lips what is in their hearts. We are then praying *with* instead of *for* those people.

I wrote Carl's breath prayer on two cards, handed one to him and kept the other. By giving him the card, I left him with a tangible reminder of a way he might help himself. Keeping a card myself let Carl know that his prayer was important to me. Also, it was my reminder to say his prayer, a reminder to pray not for but *with* him. In the weeks and months ahead, his prayer "Lead me to the light, O Lord!" would serve as a binding force between us.

Discovering Your Own Breath Prayer

The best training for teaching someone else the breath prayer is discovering your own. You can discover your prayer by following this step-by-step process.

Step 1

Sit comfortably and be calm and quiet. Close your eyes and remind yourself that you are in God's loving presence. Recall a passage from scripture that places you in the proper frame of mind. I find this line helpful: "Be still, and know that I am God" (Psalm 46:10).

Step 2

With eyes still closed, imagine that God is calling you by name. Hear God asking you: "(*Your name*), what do you want?"

Step 3

Answer God directly with whatever comes honestly from your heart. Your answer may be no more than a single word, such as *peace* or *love* or *forgiveness*. Your answer might instead be a phrase or brief sentence, such as "I want to feel your forgiveness" or "I want to understand

your love." Whatever your response, it will be at the heart
of your prayer.

Step 4

Choose your favorite name for God. (Choices people commonly make include God, Jesus, Christ, Lord, Spirit, Shepherd, Creator.)

Step 5

Combine your name for God with your answer to God's
question of "What do you want?" and you have your
prayer. For example:

What I want	Name I call God	Possible prayer
peace	God	God, let me know your peace.
love	Jesus	Jesus, let me feel your love.
rest	Shepherd	My Shepherd, let me rest in thee.

What do you do if several ideas occur? It is helpful to
write down the various possibilities and then eliminate
and/or combine ideas until you have focused your prayer.
You may "want" many things, but you can narrow your
wants down to specific needs that are basic to your spiritual well-being. Thus the question you must ask yourself
is: What do I want that will make me feel most whole?
When you achieve this feeling of wholeness, serenity
flows to all parts of your life.

Once you get at the heart of your needs, search for words
that give them expression. Then work with the words
until you have a prayer of six to eight syllables that flows
smoothly when spoken aloud or when expressed silently
as heart-thoughts.

Some prayers are most rhythmic when God's name is placed at the beginning; others require it at the end. When your prayer seems right for you, use it again and again throughout the day. Your prayer—and the ones you will lead others to discover—help answer scripture's call to pray unceasingly.

Frequently Asked Questions about the Breath Prayer

At conferences with clergy and laity who are working with the sick and dying, I always invite discussion. The following questions about the breath prayer come up wherever I go:

When people begin using the breath prayer, what happens to other prayers they may have been saying?

The breath prayer does not replace prayers they may have been saying or their ways of expressing them. In my view it is a way of completing the picture. Imagine, if you will, a new housing development where four or five houses have been built. I liken those houses to familiar forms of prayer, such as intercession, Bible reading, and private prayer time. One morning as you pass by the development you notice that all the houses have been built and the sidewalks poured, but nothing has yet been done to the yards. Though complete in themselves, the houses stand apart from one another and give the neighborhood a disjointed look. A few days later you pass by again and notice that the nursery workers have been there. Sod has been laid and shrubbery is in place. What a change! The houses are joined by greenery, and suddenly the neighborhood has a completed, unified look.

The breath prayer serves much the same purpose as the greenery around the houses in that it unites and unifies all ways of praying. No single form of prayer is weakened, changed, or neglected. Instead, each is enhanced because, as most people discover, their personal breath prayer brings a new depth and dimension to their familiar ways of praying.

How is the breath prayer different from the mantra used in non-Christian forms of meditation?

People who are given a mantra in, say, transcendental meditation are usually given it as part of a mystical ritual or ceremony and cautioned to limit its use. Typically those practicing this form of meditation focus on their mantra twice a day for twenty minutes.

There is nothing magical or mysterious about the breath prayer. It is not a chant or word or sound given to us by someone else. Nor does it involve secret ceremonies or rituals. Instead, it is a self-discovered prayer that arises naturally from within each of us as our personal response to God. Best of all, the breath prayer can be used anywhere at any time. Many of us find it to be the first step toward praying unceasingly.

I personally use my breath prayer in a variety of situations. For example, in traffic that tempts me to lay on the horn, I say my prayer instead. It has a calming influence and reminds me to respond lovingly to others. I also find the breath prayer to be a helpful means of quieting myself so that I can be more attentive to God while alone in prayer. By sitting for a time and focusing on the prayer, I feel myself moving more consciously into the presence of God.

Is the breath prayer "vain repetition"?

Whenever I hear this question, I assume the person who asks it has in mind the passage from Matthew in which Jesus warns against insincere prayer and the mistaken belief that we will be heard for our "many words" (Matt.

6:7). Certainly any prayer can be mouthed with only the lips, but the personal nature of the breath prayer makes it unlikely that we will use it in a careless or vainly repetitious manner.

Although the breath prayer is frequently repeated, it is not some magical way to get results from God. Rather, it acts as a focus and, over time, becomes as much a part of us as our own breathing.

When I was very young, I was taught that every time I heard a siren (fire, ambulance, police) I was to pray for all the people involved in the crisis situation. The length of the prayer was not stressed, only the need to respond in spirit to those in trouble. Now in my forties, I still find myself praying whenever I hear a siren. Because I have repeated this behavior over such a long period of time, it—like the breath prayer—has become second nature to me.

Why is the breath prayer so short?

The prayer is short because it flows from a basic need that can be simply expressed in a few words. The prayer should come as easily and naturally as drawing a breath, so it can't be very long. Also, the brevity of the prayer makes it easy to remember and is thus suitable for people of all ages in all kinds of circumstances. The sick and dying find the prayer especially useful because of the ease with which it can be remembered and said. Most of us find that our breath prayer takes on a singsong quality, and the words that speak of our deepest need enter the mind and heart throughout the day, no matter what else we might be doing.

How does one get into the habit of using the breath prayer?

First, you must have an interest in enriching your spiritual life; second, you must get in the habit of praying. Once you've made the conscious decision to be more attentive to your spiritual growth, you can find ways to work prayer into your daily routine.

A dentist I know began using her prayer every time she washed her hands at the office, praying for the next patient. Now she finds that she remembers it every time she washes her hands, no matter where she is. A secretary has developed the habit of praying each time her phone rings. A sales rep who spends a lot of hours in his car uses his breath prayer whenever he glances in the rearview mirror. Many people tell me they began being more attentive to their prayer life by placing a card with their prayer on the bathroom mirror as a reminder to begin each day in the presence of God. I have found that my own prayer is like a close friend who joins me while I walk, run, or ride a bike.

What can I do if I feel uncomfortable talking about the breath prayer with someone?

First discover your own breath prayer and try it for a while. Once you become comfortable with it and experience its benefits, you will feel that you are doing others a favor by introducing them to this way of praying. As I did in sharing the prayer with Carl, try to do it in a casual, conversational manner: "I've found this way of praying very helpful and maybe you will too." The person's response will let you know whether you should say more about it at that time.

What do you do if terminally ill patients ask for physical healing in their breath prayers?

There may be times when a patient responds to the question "What do you want?" by saying, "I want to be healed." If I know that a patient has a bleak prognosis, I say, "If you were healed right now, how would you feel?" "I'd feel peaceful" is a likely response. I would then suggest a prayer based on that statement. Such a prayer might be, "Let me feel your peace, O Lord." This does not deny the possibility of healing but moves the patient's focus beyond physical healing to the peace God offers no matter what occurs.

When a diagnosis of terminal illness is first made, people who are introduced to the breath prayer might focus only on healing. However, as the illness progresses, they tend to reach a stage of acceptance and seek such things as inner peace, release from this life, and an awareness of God's presence.

Is it possible that I am already using a breath prayer?

Often people call me aside at conferences to tell me that the breath prayer is not something new and that they've been using such a prayer without calling it that. As I talk with them, I usually discover that these people don't stay with a *specific* prayer for very long. Instead, they tend to alternate their prayers or have "crisis" prayers that they fall back on whenever a problem arises. I encourage those who have used a number of prayers to go back through the discovery process to find out what their most *basic* response is to God's question: "What do you really want?" Then I urge them to stick with that prayer for at least three weeks. Staying with a single prayer that expresses the person's deepest need is a proven way to focus on God's power and love.

Will my breath prayer ever change?

Yes, your prayer is likely to change over time. This is most apt to happen when you have come to some point of insight, change, or shift in your life. Whatever causes you to reflect—birth, death, marriage, divorce, job change, resolution of a problem—can alter your prayer. Often the change occurs without your giving any thought to it. One day you realize you're saying a different prayer, one that expresses the needs of your heart at that particular time and place in your life.

We need to keep in mind that prayer is a loving response to our loving Creator. As we grow and change, so, too, will our response to the abiding and unconditional love of God.

_____ *3* _____
Sharing the Breath Prayer

It was cold in Erie, Pennsylvania, that December night in 1960. I had just closed my books after many hours of studying for college exams and decided I needed a walk before going to bed. I still vividly recall the air's frosty bite, the brightness of the stars, the crunch of snow under my heavy boots. My thoughts turned to spiritual matters as I walked alone along Erie's deserted streets. I was restless and unfilled. What was I seeking? Where was I going?

That winter night I made two significant decisions: I consciously decided that I was called to be on a journey with my God and that, as the foundation of my faith life, I would use a short prayer to keep me spiritually disciplined.

I made it a point to pray often in the ensuing months. When I was going for a walk, driving, or waiting in line, I would say my short prayer. In much the same way that I was breathing without giving it conscious thought, prayer was going on spontaneously within my being. Later I learned I had discovered a natural way to pray that—though new to me—had been used through the centuries.

In some religious traditions the short prayer of praise and petition was called an ejaculatory or aspiratory prayer. An example of a breath prayer developed in the sixth and seventh centuries is the Jesus Prayer: "Lord Jesus Christ, son of God, have mercy on me, a sinner," or the shorter "Lord Jesus Christ, have mercy," or the even shorter "Jesus, mercy." I had been led to choose a more personal approach. Mine was an intimate prayer that would clarify who I was and where I stood in my relationship with God.

At the time, I was far from being ready to share the breath prayer with others. Spirituality and prayer were, for me, private matters. I had little sense of prayer being a corporate concern, something that unites us with God and one another even though we may be praying alone. When I began teaching college classes, doing campus ministry, and involving myself in adult education, I thought spirituality was much like any academic subject; it was something to be taught. My own spiritual growth brought insights that caused my thinking to change. Although some aspects of spirituality need to be taught, I now realize how much we can learn when we share spiritual experiences and how enriching the sharing of prayer can be. Since I began introducing the breath prayer to others, it has had a ripple effect. The way it has helped so many people in such a variety of circumstances has been one of the most gratifying aspects of my ministry.

Working with Shut-ins

One area of ministry where the breath prayer has been especially useful is working with shut-ins. For the most part, these are the elderly and infirm, many of whom suffer from chronic conditions that eventually require hospitalization or nursing home care. Shut-ins are often thought of as living behind the closed apartment doors in a large, impersonal city, but they are found everywhere. Sally was a shut-in who lived in a small rural community.

Stooped, frail, and in her late seventies, Sally spent most of her time in a single room of the house she had lived in for over half a century. She prided herself on having been a hard-working, resourceful woman and now stoically accepted the limitations brought about by age and illness.

On one of my visits, the matter of her failing eyesight and poor memory came up. "I can't read the Bible anymore," she admitted regretfully. "And I can't even remember my prayers very well. Without my Bible reading or my prayers, I get to feeling awful lonesome."

We discussed arrangements to get her the talking book program. Listening to the Bible and other books on tape would fill some of her lonely hours and enlarge her shrinking world. Then I said, "Sally, there's something a lot of people have found helpful and you might, too. It's a simple little prayer known as the breath prayer." After talking a bit about how to discover her prayer, Sally came up with "Lord Jesus, let me feel you with me." How fitting that petition seemed for a lonely woman hungering for spiritual nourishment.

A couple weeks later, on a return visit, I asked Sally if she was using her breath prayer. With a heavy sigh, she said, "I try, but even so short a prayer is hard to remember." I realized then that I had neglected to write the prayer down. Taking an index card from my pocket (by now they had become standard equipment), I printed, "Lord Jesus, let me feel you with me." The letters were big enough for Sally to see. I suggested that she put the card near her favorite rocker and say it over and over as she rocked. From remarks Sally had made on previous visits, I knew she had trouble with insomnia. I mentioned that the breath prayer could be used to help her fall asleep and also when she awoke in the night. As I left that day, I printed her prayer on another card and put it on the bedside table.

Before I began sharing the breath prayer with shut-ins such as Sally, I always felt a sense of inadequacy—even guilt—about my inability to be of much help. I wanted to leave something behind. Something useful. Something practical. The breath prayer proved to be the answer. When shut-ins discovered their prayer, I felt confident its repeated use would help them feel God's comforting presence and, in turn, feel less isolated and alone.

A Valuable Resource for the Church

During my years of pastoring, I came to appreciate shut-ins as a valuable resource. All of us have a need to be needed, yet too often people who have physical limitations feel they are a burden and of no use to anybody. They think they have nothing to offer when in fact they have a commodity the rest of us complain we have too little of. What is that commodity? Time. Once I recognized the value of their many uncommitted minutes and hours, I knew shut-ins could play an important part in the prayer life of the parish.

On my visits to shut-ins, I began talking about special projects and programs at the church and asked that they support them with their prayers. This developed into a network of praying people and a sense that, though unable to leave their homes, they were still an important part of the parish community.

Soon the shut-ins were not limiting themselves to praying for church events; they were praying for one another as well. At first I used individual cards on which to write the names of people and their breath prayers. I gave the cards to anyone who wanted to be involved in the prayer network. The cards expanded into a list that included eight to ten names and prayers:

Sally: *Lord Jesus, let me feel you with me.*
Leo: *Let me know your presence, Lord.*
Fran: *Father, let me feel your love. . . .*

I soon discovered that the most meaningful aspect of the prayer networking was that people felt they were praying *with* one another instead of praying *for* somebody. I then took the prayer list idea a step further and suggested we set aside a time each day when we would go over our lists and say one another's prayers. That way we would know that at a certain time (or times) of day we were united in prayer. Not as a single voice but as many voices we were following the scriptural advice to "let your requests be made known to God. And the peace of God, which passes all understanding, will keep your hearts and your minds in Christ Jesus" (Phil. 4:6–7).

If you want to begin a prayer chain (a group of people who are phoned for specific prayer requests from the congregation), consider your shut-in population as a rich resource. The prayer chain builds community and gives a sense of usefulness and purpose to parishioners who lead isolated and often lonely lives.

Working with the Hospitalized

How do you feel when you enter the hospital room of someone who is ill or dying? Some of us enter with trepidation, others with confidence. All of us enter with the hope that we can say or do something that will be of comfort.

Early in my pastoral work, I grew dissatisfied with the way I was handling my hospital ministry. I would go to a patient's room, visit a bit, say a prayer, and leave. Often I asked about the patient's condition and tried to deal with feelings—those of the patient and of family members. Rarely, though, did I talk about what was happening in the soul. Was the patient responding to the circumstance prayerfully? If so, were the prayers bringing a measure of comfort and peace? Although I wasn't exactly avoiding prayer, I never dealt with it directly.

From my own experiences of sickness and hospitalization, I remember times when I was so sick of being sick that I couldn't pray. My wish was that I either die or get well. What I had come to realize as I visited the hospitalized was that the prayers we pray when we are well often don't seem relevant to the slow process of recovery. Nor do they address the anxieties that accompany the wait for test results or the weariness and worry that are part of terminal illness.

Adam's situation was one of painful and prolonged recovery. When I first met this gentle, accepting man, he had already been flat on his back for two weeks. Ahead of him stretched another four to six weeks in that same immobile position. As I entered Adam's room, my gaze went directly to the ceiling. Colorful helium-filled balloons floated there, bright strings dangling like party streamers. Get-well cards attached to ribbons hung from the curtains, the TV, and the ceiling where Adam could see them.

Adam and I chatted for a while. He was bearing his problems with admirable patience and dignity, but understandably he often felt discouraged and depressed. As it neared time for me to leave, I said, "Adam, there's something a lot of people have found helpful in times of illness and you might find it helpful, too. It's called the breath prayer."

Adam was interested in hearing more so I led him through the steps outlined in chapter 2. I asked him what he would say if God asked, "What do you want, Adam?"

"Peace," he responded instantly. "I'd like to feel peaceful while I'm lying here."

The prayer Adam came up with was "O God, let me feel your peace." The flow of the words didn't seem quite right, so we turned it around and he liked it better as "Let me feel your peace, O God." I printed his prayer in large letters on both sides of an index card and hung it like a mobile from one of the ribbons attached to the TV.

"Say the prayer as often as you like," I said. "Let it become a companion during the day and when you wake up in the night." I told him my usual time for prayer was the same time the nurses took morning temperatures.

"Say your prayer while you wait with the thermometer in your mouth," I suggested, "and I'll be saying it along with you." I also recommended that Adam share the prayer with his family, and perhaps they would use it when they got up in the morning and also when they gathered for meals. He liked the idea that it was a way for all of us to be praying together.

It was three weeks before I saw Adam again. On my first visit after returning from my travels, I noticed the small card on which I'd written his prayer had been replaced by a larger one with fancily printed letters and a colorful border. Adam's daughter had contributed the artwork and also written the prayer on small cards that the family kept at home so they would be reminded to pray with him.

Adam was able to come up with his own breath prayer, but I've encountered situations where the hospitalized are so ill they have a difficult time focusing their thoughts. I then ask if they have a favorite hymn or line from scripture. Here are some breath prayers that have evolved in this way: "Just a closer walk with thee, O Lord." "The Lord is my Shepherd, I shall not want." "My soul yearns for you, O Lord." "Rock of ages, let me find myself in thee." "Be still and know that I am God."

Facing Surgery

Martha and her husband, Bob, were coming from a small town to a Birmingham city hospital where they would be six hours away from home, family, and friends. Their pastor knew me and, because he couldn't be there himself, called to ask if I would meet with them. "They're in their late thirites," he said, "and Martha's scheduled for brain surgery. . . ."

The call had come about seven on a Tuesday evening. A short while later I was walking down the hall toward hospital room 408, my thoughts still processing the infor-

47

mation I had been given over the phone. Martha's survival prognosis was fifty-fifty. Back home were a concerned parish and a family of three very worried children.

When I walked into the room, Bob and Martha were holding hands. There was panic in Bob's eyes; Martha just looked sad. Although they knew nothing of me except that I was their pastor's friend, Martha talked readily and knowledgeably about her surgery. It seemed that in the telling she was distancing herself from the situation, or perhaps she was just taking the opportunity to talk about it as she had never done before. She was in control and giving information rather than hearing it from someone else.

In time, the conversation got around to their feelings, especially hopes and fears about their family. Among us there was the unspoken awareness that this could be Martha's last night of earthly life. Huddled behind the drawn curtain that separated us from Martha's roommate, we celebrated communion with tears very near. I called to mind the Last Supper and how emotion-filled it must have been.

I prepared to leave, assuring them that I would be there in the morning when Martha was taken to surgery. Then I found myself saying, "There's a simple little prayer that many people have found helpful. . . ." Martha expressed interest, and the prayer she discovered for herself was "Father, let me feel your peace."

"Let it help you relax," I told her. "When you're going to sleep, repeat it over and over in a light, singsongy way." I pointed out that some people find it helpful to vary the emphasis. For example:

"*Father*, let me feel your peace."
"Father, *let* me feel your peace."
"Father, let *me* feel your peace . . ."

Before leaving, I suggested they call their children and

share the prayer with them. Martha said she would also call some people in her parish so they could use the prayer, too. Martha and Bob were holding hands again as I walked out. I heard them taking turns saying, "Father, let me feel your peace."

At five-thirty the next morning, I was back at the hospital. Martha took comfort in knowing that her children and parishioners back home were praying with her. Both she and her husband tried to be calm, but as the hour for surgery approached, it was obvious they were becoming scattered in their thoughts. At such a time, I find it best to be directive:

"We'll say a prayer now. I'll ask for blessing and guidance on the part of the medical team and for peace and strength for you all. When they come to take Martha to surgery, Bob, you walk with her as far as they will let you go. Then give her a kiss, assure her of your love for her, and whisper her prayer in her ear.

"Martha, when Bob whispers your prayer, begin saying it and try to keep it going. Even though you're drowsy from the medication, you'll still remember it. It may be the first thing you remember when you wake up, and it will seem as if you've been saying it all the while. I believe that's because the Holy Spirit prays for us even when we are not able to do it for ourselves. Just trust."

They came to take Martha then. I turned to Bob who was pale and distraught. Quietly but firmly I repeated the instructions: "Kiss her, tell her you love her, whisper the prayer to her." Then making the sign of the cross on Martha's forehead, I spoke the words from our baptismal ceremony: "Remember, Martha, you are signed as Christ's own forever."

Bob and I met for breakfast in the hospital cafeteria.

"The kids will be having a hard time in school today," he said. "Sharing their mom's prayer with them was a good idea. I think they'll be too busy praying to pay attention to the teacher!" We both laughed.

Later, in the surgical waiting room, there came that moment known well to anyone who has ever spent time waiting with family members: we were "talked out." But often family members feel obligated to make conversation anyway because I am there doing something for them. At such times I suggest we sit quietly for a while and say the person's breath prayer to ourselves.

I find this time of silence to be like an oasis for the weary traveler. As I sit in prayer, I visualize God's peace and love moving among the people present. Sometimes I let my gaze wander around the room and, one-by-one, pray for each person. Grace and power come from a loving God, and in this moment I am often astounded at how an atmosphere that had been charged with tension changes to one of calm.

It has been nine years since I sat with Bob in that waiting room. Today Martha is a healthy, active woman filled with gratitude for the years she has been granted.

I remember the experience with Martha and Bob so vividly because it was the first of many times that I have shared the breath prayer with patients preparing for surgery. Over the years, I have seen people take charge of their breath prayer and come up with new and creative ways to share it. A case in point is Marilyn.

Marilyn was a member of my parish, and I knew she was using the breath prayer as part of her daily discipline. When I visited her the night before she was scheduled for surgery, she said she had told her family and the prayer chain members to pray her prayer with her. As her visit ended, I reminded her to use her prayer just before surgery. "More than likely," I said, "it will be the first thing you remember when you wake up."

"I've already taken care of that," Marilyn replied. "This afternoon the nurse from the recovery room came by to introduce herself. She said when I surfaced, she wanted me to see a familiar face. I talked about my prayer and printed it on a card for her. I asked her to whisper it to me while I'm in recovery, and she said she would."

Stories like Marilyn's affirm the helpfulness of the breath prayer and the need people have for that simple little something they can hold onto in times of stress.

The Comatose Patient

The first coma victim I used the breath prayer with was Charlie, a fifty-two-year-old businessman. Charlie had been in a car accident, and when I first saw him, he had already been comatose for several weeks. Even so, I held his hand and talked to him as though he were conscious.

How much do the comatose hear? feel? sense? Medical research indicates that it may be much more than was once believed. A close friend who was in a coma recalls that he felt horribly frustrated when he could not "argue back" with two doctors who stood beside his hospital bed talking about him as though he were already dead. Since we don't know how aware the comatose are, it's extremely important for us to be positive in their presence. Conversations should be no different than if they were fully alert.

How do you talk to someone who does not respond? to someone you are not sure even hears you? At first you may feel foolish carrying on a one-sided conversation, but if you keep in mind that *your words just might be getting through*, it's worth risking a little foolishness.

I talk about such everyday matters as the weather and what's happening in the community and wider world. If the coma victim has a love of poetry or of fiction, I often read aloud from a favorite work. Frequently I try to communicate with music. I find out the person's musical tastes and come equipped with a tape recorder and double earphones. Some of my most loving and prayerful times with coma victims and the sick in general have come when we've listened to music together.

One day after Charlie and I had been listening to music, I said, "Charlie, I'm going to tell you about something that a lot of people have found helpful. It's called the breath prayer." I went on to say that coma victims find their thoughts scattered, so it's hard to remember long prayers, even one as familiar as the Lord's Prayer. "The breath prayer is a short prayer of praise and petition," I explained. "The praise comes from calling God by name. What do you usually call God? Since you can't answer, let's just say 'Lord Jesus.'" (I always use "Lord Jesus" for the comatose because most people carry a mental picture of Jesus, but it may be difficult to visualize God.)

I continued, "Imagine Jesus standing in front of you asking, 'Charlie, what do you want?' How would you answer? I'll say you might answer Jesus by saying, 'Let me feel your strength.'" (I consistently use the word *feel* because it focuses coma victims' attention on their own sensing. Then on their behalf I ask for strength or power or life.)

"Now you have a breath prayer, Charlie," I said. "The prayer is 'Lord Jesus, let me feel your strength.' When we're together, I'll sometimes say your prayer out loud to you. Other times we'll just be together in silence saying the prayer to ourselves. By saying over and over, 'Lord Jesus, let me feel your strength; Lord Jesus, let me feel your strength,' the prayer will become a song in your heart. When you can't pray it for yourself, the Holy Spirit will do it for you, and so will I."

From then on I always began my visits to Charlie by introducing myself and saying, "Let's sit together while I repeat your prayer out loud for two minutes." That allowed for twenty-five to thirty repetitions and possibly some communication of time-sense to help reorient him. I would then say, "Let's sit in silence for two more minutes. I'll say the prayer in my heart, and you do the same."

After I told Charlie's family about the prayer, they shared in it as well. I suggested that they repeat the prayer for a minute (about fifteen times) at the beginning of their visit and again at the end. Often families feel self-conscious doing this, so I introduce the prayer and we all say it aloud fifteen times. Once families have done it, they find the practice easier to repeat.

I would like to report that Charlie came out of his coma, but he did not. He died quietly, and I never knew whether he was aware of the many prayers said both for and with him. I do know, however, that the breath prayer was a unifying force for his family.

The story of another coma victim I ministered to ended differently. Fred was a single man in his forties whose nearest relatives lived a considerable distance away. I first met Fred the day after he entered the hospital with a serious head injury. Immediately I took his hand and told him that he might be feeling disoriented and unable to remember any prayers. Possibly, I said, he would remember the first line and no more. Even if he could recall only "Our Father," that was enough. Then I proceeded much the same way I had with Charlie. After explaining the breath prayer to Fred, I came up with one for him.

Six weeks after Fred went into his coma, he came out of it. Eventually he regained his health, and he came to see me several months after his recovery. Obviously uneasy, he said, "I have to ask you something. When I was in the hospital, did you say it was okay just to say the beginning of the Lord's Prayer and not to worry about the whole thing?"

"Yes, I did. It was the first time I saw you."

Fred shook his head in amazement. "Well, I remember that! And I just wanted to thank you."

Fred's experience was a welcome affirmation that at least in some cases we do reach through the veil of the coma.

The Stroke Patient

One day I was talking with a friend who had suffered a stroke. Although he had made a remarkable recovery, he still had some difficulty with his speech. Our discussion brought us around to the breath prayer, and I asked Harry if he wanted to share his with me. He seemed embarrassed and tried to speak but could only stammer.

"Harry," I said, "do you say the breath prayer over and over in your head like we've talked about doing, but when you try to say it out loud, you can't quite get it out?"

He nodded. "N . . . no matter what I'm doing . . . it . . . it's always there inside me."

It didn't matter that Harry couldn't say the words to his prayer out loud because it was serving him very well indeed. It had become a song in his heart.

4
Karen and Her Prayer

My introduction to Karen was through her husband, Jim. One day he called my office, and even as he introduced himself, I sensed the desperation in his voice. "Would you be willing to help us the way you helped Carl?" he asked.

"You must mean Carl Tukker." He had died about a month before. I had been part of the active, though unofficial, support group who had ministered to Carl and his family.

"That's the one," Jim said. "You see . . ." He paused as though trying to swallow away the tightness in his throat. "My wife Karen has cancer." I got the impression he had not totally accepted the fact of her illness and that admitting it to me was making it more of a reality.

"Can you tell me a bit about Karen's situation?" I knew I was on emotionally painful ground, but a little more information about her illness would give me a better idea of how to proceed.

"She has . . ." I heard him turn away from the phone and call, "Honey, what's the name of what you have?" His question let me know that I would need to get some information on my own about Karen's disease. I find that this is often the case and have a doctor and nurse with whom I consult. These friends give me an idea of how the disease can be expected to progress, and they suggest practical things to do—things that I share with the family.

Karen's diagnosis was adenocarcinoma. "She's had three operations," Jim said. "Now the doctors say there's nothing more they can do for her." The flatness in his voice told me that a feeling of hopelessness had set in.

"Let's arrange a time for me to come by and visit with you and Karen," I suggested. "If you have children, it would be best if I came when they're not around. That way we'll be freer to talk."

"We have two girls in their teens and a son who's eight," Jim said. "They'll be in school tomorrow."

We made an appointment for the following morning. That evening I called my two friends in the medical profession and asked about adenocarcinoma. From Robert, I learned that in Karen's case fluid would build up in the body and drainage would be necessary. Death would probably come from suffocation due to excess fluid in the lungs. Pain could be fairly well controlled with the use of drugs. Nancy informed me that some sort of home nursing service would be available for Karen if she should need it.

The First Meeting

Karen and Jim lived in a large townhouse complex on the edge of the city. All the units looked the same, and each had its own little courtyard. I was looking for a place with a green door that faced a playground. A lot of units fit that description. As I drove around looking for the right house number, I grew increasingly anxious.

Meeting someone who is terminally ill is always a challenge. I feel a sense of both expectancy and hesitation. Early in my ministry, I would sometimes secretly wish the person wouldn't be home. Or if it was a hospital visit, I would hope the individual was in X-ray, and I could just leave my card. (Of course the patient would assume I was so busy I couldn't come back that day!) Over time I've faced up to my feelings about sickness and death. When I accepted my own mortality and grew comfortable with it,

I became more willing to share myself and my time with those whose bodies were failing them. However, on that day while I hunted for the residence of Jim and Karen Hammer, some discomfort remained. I was more than a little uneasy.

Jim, a tall, solidly built man in his late thirties, greeted me. I followed him through a narrow entry that led to the living room where Karen was tilted back in a recliner chair in front of the window. I first noticed her luxuriant, reddish-blonde hair—hair that I would later learn was a wig. She had lost her own hair after having chemotherapy treatments. Although Karen's skin was pale, her blue eyes were lively, and her warm smile helped put me at ease. By contrast, Jim seemed nervous and distracted, behavior I have found to be common in such situations. Often patients come to terms with a bleak prognosis before those closest to them accept it. That is one of the reasons it is so important to involve the whole family in discussion and prayer.

We went through the usual getting-acquainted conversation, exchanging information about jobs and families. Jim was a postal worker who'd arranged to get time off to be home with his wife and help with the children. I talked about Eleanor and our two children, where we lived, and my particular ministry. The Hammers were churchgoing people but said the church they belonged to was so large that their pastor didn't have much time to give to individuals. "When he does come, he seems very uncomfortable," Jim said. "He brings communion, says a quick prayer, and makes a hasty exit."

Then the moment came—as it always does—to get to the matter at hand. It can be an awkward or a liberating time, depending upon how you feel about confronting the realities of illness and impending death. My experience has been that people really want to talk about their illness;

they want to "get the story out." And so with a gentleness that I hoped conveyed the concern I felt, I said, "Tell me about your cancer, Karen."

What followed was a story that took about half an hour in the telling. First there was the lump, then the biopsy, then surgery. More lumps, another surgery, and the removal of an organ. A week later another removal. "It all happened so fast," Karen said. "One day the doctor scheduled a visit for both Jim and me. 'Is there something you always wanted to do?' he asked. 'Or is there someplace you always wanted to go?' He said that if there was, we should do it and do it soon. The disease was progressing rapidly, and he didn't know how much time I had left."

The one place Karen had always wanted to visit was Hawaii, so the family took a trip. That had been just the month before, and I looked through the pile of photos they had taken. "We had to get a loan to be able to go," Jim said, "but it was sure worth it."

Karen's Breath Prayer

There was a break in the conversation, and I asked what Carl Tukker's mother had said that prompted them to call me. "She said that you helped them in a lot of ways," Karen replied. "But one thing that helped especially was something she called the breath prayer."

I then explained the concept of the breath prayer and how it helps us be more attentive to God's presence in our lives; how it tends to move us away from the *whys* and *what ifs* and helps us get on with living out whatever time we have left. I shared that from my own experiences with sickness and surgery—and from what others had told me of theirs—the breath prayer helps us ride with the pain instead of fighting it. Fighting pain only makes it worse.

"The breath prayer can be like a boat that carries us across the river between this life and risen life," I said. "I believe that when we move through the physical door of death, Jesus, along with all those loved ones who have made the passage before us, will be there saying our breath prayer."

I grew silent then and waited for a response. Without hesitation both Jim and Karen decided they wanted to use the prayer. Karen's yes was so decisive that clearly she wanted to get on with her living. Jim, I believe, would have tried anything at that point. Turning to Karen, I said, "What do you normally call God? Do you use Father? Lord? Jesus?"

After a moment's thought, Karen said, "Just 'God,' I guess."

"All right. Let's be silent while you imagine God being right here in front of you asking, 'Karen, what do you want?' Jim, you and I will sit in silence, aware that God is here with us." (Remember that scripture tells us "where two or three are gathered in my name, there am I in the midst of them" [Matt. 18:20].)

When the minute was up, I looked at Karen and asked, "Did anything come to you?"

She nodded. "Yes, I heard God speaking to me very clearly."

"What did God say?"

"Come to me, my child, and I will give you peace and rest."

Jim's eyes bugged out, but I acted as if Karen's experience was in no way out of the ordinary—which it was not. "How are you going to respond?" I asked.

There was a moment of silence during which Karen closed her eyes. When she opened them, she said with great certainty, "Let me come to you, O God."

"Let me come to you, O God," I repeated. "That's beautiful, Karen. Some people have a difficult time coming up with their prayer. You are blessed in having heard the Lord so clearly. Rejoice in that." Turning my attention to Jim, I said, "You can use Karen's prayer, too. It will be a way for both of you to share something even when you're apart. But remember what the prayer is: *Karen is asking to be led to God.*"

Jim's eyes misted over; he looked at Karen and back at me. Then, with a deep sigh of resignation, he said, "Yes, I heard that."

It was nearing time for me to leave. The hour or so we had spent together had been good and productive but emotionally draining. "Let's get back together soon," I suggested. "In the meantime, the two of you will have a chance to accustom yourselves to the prayer. It's probably not a good idea to involve the kids until both of you have lived with it for a while."

I wrote the prayer on cards—one for Jim and one for Karen—and recommended that they leave one there on the table where they would see it often. "Say the prayer whenever you think of it," I said. "Karen, let it go round and round in your head while you're resting or trying to fall asleep. Jim, you might want to use it when you're away from Karen; for instance, when you go back to work or are out buying groceries. The prayer will be a way of staying in contact with her."

We said our good-byes then, and I promised to return in two days. As I closed the green door behind me and walked to my car, "Let me come to you, O God" played over and over in my head.

The Family Gets Involved

The Hammers lost no time putting the breath prayer to use. When Jim returned to his work at the post office, he told Karen he would be saying her prayer at lunch and during his breaks. Karen took note of his schedule and set her alarm so they could be praying together. The plan gave Karen a feeling that she was taking some positive action. It also gave her something to anticipate doing during the long and lonely days.

A couple weeks after Karen and Jim began using the prayer, their children became involved. On one of my visits to the Hammer household, I got Elaine, Barbara, and Jeff together and told them about the prayer. I had printed it on self-adhering stickers and gave some to each of them. "You may want to stick the prayer on your notebooks," I said. "Each time you change class and take out a new notebook, you'll be reminded to pray for your mother."

At first the girls weren't interested. They were still avoiding the fact that their mother had a terminal illness. I also sensed their hesitation to make a commitment to pray for someone else with such regularity. That's when I suggested they take one of the stickers and put it on their dresser mirror. "You may just want to say the prayer when you get up in the morning," I said. "And maybe again when you go to bed at night."

Unlike his teenage sisters, eight-year-old Jeff found the prayer to be a neat idea and began using it right away. Karen, meanwhile, was growing more attentive to her family's schedule away from home. A clock in their hallway chimed on the hour. She knew that her daughters changed classes every hour and that her son probably changed subjects. So every time the clock chimed, she remembered to say her breath prayer and to pray for each of her children.

Building Identity

Eventually Karen was confined almost totally to her recliner. She could be up only about fifteen minutes at a time, three or four times a day. Otherwise her world revolved around the chair. Each time I came I noticed more things within reach of it.

I recall coming to visit on a particularly beautiful day

when it was warm but not yet hot and flowers were blooming everywhere. I waved to the Hammer children who were outside and then knocked on the door. "Who is it?" Karen snapped, obviously not in the best of moods. When I identified myself, she said, "Oh, good. Come in."

Upon seeing Karen, I was taken aback. When it came to appearance, she was a proud person, and this was the first time I had seen her bald. "Today, all you get is the real me," she said. "No glamour. Just a dying person."

What had caused this response? Pulling up a chair so we were sitting close, I said, "Want to tell me what's bothering you?"

"I feel stupid even talking about it," she answered self-consciously. "I know she didn't mean it. I know none of them mean it."

"Who are you talking about?"

"Jim and the kids."

"I think we better start from the beginning," I said. "What happened to trigger all this?"

Karen took a deep breath and began her story. "Yesterday afternoon I was waiting for Elaine to come home from school. I thought we could have some time alone because Barbara was at band and Jeff was off with friends. Elaine came home happy and was telling me about her day. 'Oh, Mom,' she said, 'I heard the best joke. It's so funny it'll kill you. . . !' Suddenly she realized what she'd said. She burst into tears and ran upstairs. I couldn't get her to come down. Later when she came to dinner, she avoided looking at me. Finally after we'd eaten, she gave me a hug and said, 'I'm sorry, Mom.' "

Karen shook her head as though she were terribly weary of it all. "This incident with Elaine brought things to a head for me. I'm no longer a wife who can help Jim with the family . . . or a mother my kids can even share a joke with . . . I'm . . . just a dying person."

I could do nothing at the moment but listen. That was important, though, because Karen had admitted her feelings. She expressed the sentiments of many who are terminally ill. When they cannot carry out the role that had once defined them, they suffer a serious loss of identity. One of our tasks, then, is to help the family see how critical it is that the ill person still have a role to play.

At this stage in her illness, Karen was very weak. She spent most of her day in the recliner in the living room where Jim moved it so she could see both into the kitchen and out the large picture window that faced the playground. He recognized how important it was for her not to be set apart someplace where she would have no contact with household activity.

I asked Karen what she enjoyed doing for her family before she got sick. She said she had liked to set a beautiful table for dinner. We talked about that and how it still might be something she was able to do.

Karen began by asking the family to clear the table completely before they left for the day. She then used her "up" time to get the table ready for dinner. On one trip, she put the dishes and silver out. On another, she got flowers from the courtyard or made an artful arrangement from objects around the house. Before long the children anticipated seeing Mom's "decoration of the day."

Karen began to do other little things as well. She could still fold clothes if someone put the laundry basket near her chair. She made a list of all family members and began writing notes to them. When she noticed that the strain of preparing meals was getting to Jim and the girls, she wrote out creative menus for them.

People confined to their homes or hospital rooms need mental stimulation. Without it they soon discover they have little to talk about with family members and visitors. Books and other printed material have always been a source of stimulation; however, many ill people find it difficult to concentrate on the printed word, have problems with vision, or are unable to hold up a book. Television is a blessing in that it brings the world to those who cannot be out in it. Karen turned to TV to stay informed about current events and had a schedule of programs she watched during the day. In the evening, the entire family sometimes gathered in the living room to watch a show. This gave them something to share and enjoy together.

When I worked with Karen and Jim, video cassette recorders were not yet commonplace. Had they been, I would have suggested some of the creative uses I have seen other seriously ill patients put them to. For Sam who loved history, I found series upon series of biographies and historical documentaries in the library. Barbara, a woman in her early forties, began watching movies of particular stars. She tried to get the earliest movie a star made and then go on to watch the movies in the order they were filmed. Bonnie was too ill to care for her four-year-old son, but while he was at the sitter's house, she was able to tape his favorite shows. At night the boy crawled into bed with her, and they watched his favorite programs. Because Bonnie was unable to be up and about with her son, watching the shows and talking about them became the focal point of their time together. I'm certain that with access to a VCR, Karen, too, would have found ways to use it for the benefit of herself and her family.

The Brown Paper Bag

Karen had been a very successful salesperson with a cosmetics company. At the end of my visits to her at home, she often handed me a brown paper bag. When I opened it later, I would discover a selection of products for myself and the family. A few times it held a five-dollar bill and a note telling me that the money was to help pay for the gas expense of coming to see her.

Although I felt uncomfortable taking the bag, I recognized that Karen needed to thank me, and this was her way of doing it. But on one of my visits we had a conversation that changed all that.

It was a clear, bright Saturday morning. The kids were outside swimming, and I sat talking with Jim and Karen in the living room. We had been reviewing our time together and how all our lives had changed in the past year. It was an easy conversation, and in the course of it Karen said, "Ron, I don't know how I can ever repay you for what you've brought to our family and to me."

"I do," I replied immediately.

"You do?" Jim and Karen responded in unison, obviously surprised by my quick response.

"Karen," I said, "when you enter into the risen life, I fully expect that you will help me with my work. No one knows for sure what happens after this life, but I do know that here on earth our prayer unites us. And it is my belief that when we pass through death's door, we will still be united by prayer." It was one of those moments in my ministry when I felt I had been gifted by God. My response to Karen had come so readily and so naturally that I didn't feel the words were really mine. They were just there.

I'll never foget Karen's eyes and the way she looked at me. It must have been one of those "Aha!" moments because she immediately said, "That's a deal, Ron."

After that I never got another brown bag.

A Gift

About five years after Karen died, I was working with Marge, a woman in her late forties who learned that her days were ending. She was a vigorous, take-charge kind of woman who had built up her own real estate company and was a leader in the community. One night in her hospital room, we were talking about the breath prayer, and she

was having a difficult time coming up with one that satisfied her. The problem seemed to be that she wanted everything and couldn't settle on a single petition. I was getting
frustrated because she was talking on and on without
focusing on her illness or the matter at hand. In desperation, I finally said, "Marge, let's just take two minutes in
silence. That will help you get calm enough to hear the
prayer that's trying to surface. It will be what the Spirit is
already praying within you."

We entered into the silence, and I prayed that Marge
would be led to a peaceful acceptance of her illness and the
lack of control she now had over her life. At the end of the
two minutes, I asked, "Did you hear anything, Marge?"

"Yes . . .," she said with a kind of tentative amazement.
"Yes, I did." She paused as though needing time to think
about her experience before going on. "My thoughts were
whirling about, and all kinds of things were coming to
mind. Suddenly I felt peaceful and . . . well . . . quiet. It
was a different kind of feeling that's hard to put into words.
Then, clear as anything, I heard a prayer. But it wasn't just
that I *heard* the prayer; I felt it, too. It was as though
someone said it into my whole body, not just my ear."

"What did you hear?"

"It's strange," Marge mused, "because it's not something I would have come up with myself."

"Yes?" I persisted.

What I heard was "Let me come to you, O God."

It was Karen's prayer.

5

Journey into Death

About the time I began working with Carl Tukker, Dr. Elisabeth Kübler-Ross came out with a book titled *On Death and Dying*. In it, she wrote that people who are dying tend to go through five psychological stages: denial, anger, bargaining, depression, and acceptance. Not everyone goes through all the stages; the ones who do may not go through them in a neat, sequential order. Some have great trouble reaching acceptance and a few never do. Others who have had a long, painful illness may not only accept death but desperately wish for it. Being aware of the stages is a great help in understanding the journey into death and knowing how to be supportive and comforting to people at every stage.

While working with the sick and dying, I have found similarities between the psychological stages detailed by Kübler-Ross and the stages we move through on our spiritual journey. In my book *The Hunger of the Heart*, I wrote about the stages on the spiritual journey and how, as we grow spiritually, there comes a time of "giving power over." When we cease struggling to be in control, a shift of consciousness occurs wherein we are willing to accept the process. We realize that there is no particular place we must "get to"; there is only a life to live.

I was poignantly reminded of this need to take life as it comes as I prepared to write this chapter. While going through my notes and files, I came across a snapshot of Karen and Jim. It was taken about three months before Karen died, and for a long time I had kept it on my office bulletin board as a reminder of them. I turned the picture over and reread what was written on the back—their names, the date, and the message: "We learned to live, and we learned to die. Thanks."

The message brought back memories of how, in the time I had spent with Karen and Jim, the three of us had learned to live. Together we learned to live in the knowledge that life is precious and fleeting. As husband and wife, they learned to live in the midst of suffering and uncertainty and the knowledge that they were no longer in control. They understood that there was no place for them to "get to." There was only a life to live, however long that might be.

The Difficulty of Accepting

I have found the breath prayer to be very useful in helping me discover where patients are on their journey toward death. For example, when Karen said that she heard God calling and responded with "Let me come to you, O God," I had little doubt that she had already moved to the acceptance stage.

It was also obvious that Jim was trying to accept, but he was not yet able to. He was still denying the seriousness of his wife's illness and angry that this terrible thing was happening to them. His denial and anger often made it difficult for Karen to communicate with him and their children.

It is very common to find cases in which the sick person has accepted the reality of dying but says, "I can't die yet. My (*spouse, child, parent*) isn't ready for me to leave." Sometimes this presents problems, as it did with Karen and her parents. On one of my visits to her, she said, "Ron, my mother and father are driving me crazy."

I was surprised because Karen had previously told me

that she seldom saw her parents, even though they lived in the same area. "So, tell me," I said, "what's going on?"

"They're here to see me *every* day!" Karen shook her head and sighed wearily. "They stay for hours at a time and say nothing except how I'm going to get well and that I shouldn't worry because soon everything's going to be all right."

It was clear what was happening. The parents were still in the denial stage, and their daughter had moved past that to acceptance. Karen hadn't analyzed it in that way; she just knew that the too-frequent, overly long visits couldn't continue. "Do you think your parents believe you have cancer?" I asked.

"They know I have it," Karen replied, "but they act as if it's like a cold. Give it a little time, and it will go away. It's incredible. I can't mention anything about my disease in front of them. They simply refuse to see me as I am."

About three months prior to this conversation, I had suggested to both Karen and Jim that they read *On Death and Dying*. Often, though, it's difficult for the seriously ill (as well as distraught relatives) to concentrate long enough to absorb lengthy written material, so I talked to Karen about the stages and how she and her parents were at different places. Karen came to see that her parents were struggling with their guilt over paying so little attention to her and her family in the past. They were trying to make up for lost time and in the process were creating problems for Karen.

As Karen expressed her thoughts and feelings, she had other insights. She understood that her parents couldn't face up to their own mortality so, of course, they wouldn't even consider that a child of theirs might be dying. They also had a long history of being avoiders. They pretended issues weren't there instead of dealing with them. Although Karen was not emotionally close to her parents, she did love them. It was the daily visits she couldn't tolerate.

I asked Karen if she wanted me to talk to her parents. She said she would like that and at this point they would probably do anything she asked of them. They contacted me within a few days, and we made an appointment to meet at the church. Over the next couple of weeks, we met three times. In the course of our discussions, they came to an understanding of the dying process and an awareness that they had been denying the seriousness of Karen's illness. They wanted me to know that they were acting out of love and doing what every good mom and dad should do: be with their child.

Together we agreed that they should visit Karen once a week and telephone one other time. I suggested that during their visits they ask Karen how she was doing and then listen as she told them. I let them know that I recognized how hard the reality of Karen's illness was for them, but it was something they had to face.

The new visiting arrangement worked out better than anyone anticipated. In fact, a couple weeks later Karen invited her parents to dinner, and everyone had a great time. Both surprise and pleasure were in her voice as she told me about that evening and how good it was to be together.

She's Dying, Isn't She?

From the time of Jim's initial phone call to me, he had never actually denied Karen's illness. But a part of him still said it wasn't fatal. Somehow Karen was going to lick this thing.

From time to time I made an effort to talk privately with Jim just as I sometimes came by to talk alone with Karen. On one particular morning, Jim and I were sitting in the courtyard of their townhouse. He looked especially tired and tense as he gazed into the distance at something only he seemed able to see. Then in a barely audible voice, he murmured, "She's dying, isn't she?"

Even though the three of us had been talking about Karen's impending death for months, this was the first time Jim had brought the matter up on his own. Occasionally he had shed a few tears when he was with me, but never in front of Karen. He felt that he had to maintain a brave front for her and the children.

"Yes, Jim, she is dying," I said quietly. "What are you feeling that makes you ask that question now?"

His body sagged in the chair. "I guess I finally had to admit it to myself. It's real. It won't go away. It's not a bad dream. I won't wake up and find that Karen is like she was." Then he began to cry.

"You've held those tears back a long while, brother," I said. "It's time you let them fall." He held his head in his hands while great, gasping sobs fought their way up from deep inside him and shook his entire body. As his hurt and rage and sorrow spilled forth in tears, I sat silently beside him. I have found it is important at such a moment to simply accept the tears, even though I might feel compelled to say, "Oh, it'll be all right."

Silent acceptance is both honest and comforting. After Jim had cried himself out and regained his composure, I said, "Do you remember those stages that people move through in the process of giving up their physical lives? The book I asked you and Karen to read talked about them."

"Oh, yeah, the book," he said. "I read it, but I don't remember much of what it said."

"Considering the stress you're under, that's understandable," I assured him. "I just mentioned the stages because I think you and Karen are now at the same one. She has accepted her illness and so have you. That doesn't mean you won't ever again be angry about it or think it's a dream or try to strike a bargain with God. What it does mean is that you've faced reality, and there's something freeing about that." I paused a moment, letting what I'd said take hold before I continued. "Remember how hard it was for you to use Karen's prayer at first? 'Let me come to you, O God' was her way of saying that she was already in the acceptance stage. Now that you're where she is, her prayer will have new meaning for you each time you say it."

We talked a bit more, and I told him that he needed to tell Karen what had happened. "Do you want me to stay around?" I asked. "Or would you be more comfortable doing it alone?"

"Please stay," Jim said. "I might start to cry again, and you'll have to do the talking."

Witnessing what took place between Jim and Karen was a privileged experience. I looked on as two people who had shared deeply in their years of married love now shared on a level so deep and intimate that it became a sanctified and grace-filled segment of time. As their conversation ended, Karen spoke with tears shimmering in her eyes. "Now we can *really* talk with each other, Jim. I've been waiting."

Easing the Passage

Sometimes when people have accepted the finality of their illness, they just want to get the dying over with. My mother-in-law was such a person. One day she said to Eleanor, "I wish I could just die." She had clung to life through years of health problems and painful dialysis treatment. But now she realized that her time was limited, and she felt a sense of uselessness while waiting out her days.

An inspired idea came to Eleanor one morning in prayer. That day, while driving her mother to a dialysis appointment, Eleanor said, "Mother, two things in your life have always been very important—your prayer life and your children. One way to feel your life has more purpose would be to pray for each one of us kids on a specific day of the week. How do you feel about that?"

Her mother liked the idea and seemed relieved to have something that would give meaning to her days. Thus it was established that on a given day of the week, she would pray especially for one child and that child's family if there was one. On Monday she prayed for Mark. Tuesday was Mary Kay's day. Wednesday she prayed for Eleanor, Paul, Anne, and me and so on from the oldest to the youngest of the six children. Sunday was for herself and Eleanor's father. Not only did the prayer plan give meaning to Mom's days, but we found that on Wednesdays we were thinking of her in a special way. The children in the family were spread all around the country, and everyone had tended to call on the weekend. Instead, we all tried to call on our prayer day, a day that we often found brought unique manifestations of God's love and care for us.

My mother-in-law had been a very spiritual woman throughout her life. She would often image herself with Jesus and experience God's abiding presence. Once at a family reunion, both she and my father-in-law said they wanted to plan their funerals while all the children were together. In the course of the discussion, Mom said that her favorite recollection of Jesus was at the table with his friends. The scripture she wanted read at her funeral was from the Last Supper discourse of the Gospel of John. How fitting that seemed because having the entire family gathered around the table for a meal was one of her greatest pleasures.

Mom's illness progressed, and she was in a lot of pain from continuing dialysis. On top of that, she suffered a broken collarbone. Eleanor had flown to St. Louis to be with her, and as often happened when they were together, their conversation turned to matters of the spirit. "Are you able to image yourself with Jesus?" Eleanor asked.

When her mother said that she was, Eleanor asked where she saw herself.

"On the cross," her mother responded.

Because Mom had always had such a devotion to Mary, the mother of Jesus, Eleanor suggested that she imagine herself taken down from the cross and placed in Mary's arms. "See Mary holding you the way she held Jesus when he was taken down from the cross," Eleanor said. The idea was immediately appealing to her mother. Subsequently when she was in a lot of pain, she was able to call forth the image and feel Mary's tenderness and concern.

Eleanor and I later discussed what had taken place, and I became aware of the subtle but significant shift that had occurred in Mom's thoughts. She had gone from visualizing the gathering of friends at the Last Supper to the solitariness on the cross with the dying Jesus to the comfort and intimacy of being held in Mary's loving arms. Not long after Eleanor's visit, her mother made the decision to go off dialysis. Eleanor returned to St. Louis, and the day after she arrived, her mother died. It was Pentecost Sunday.

My mother-in-law's journey into death was unique, as are all such journeys, yet she typifies the experience of those who have a deep sense of God's presence and action in their lives. People who use imagery and can visualize themselves with Jesus find solace in their final days and their passage into risen life is eased.

A Time to Die

"To every thing there is a season, and a time to every purpose under the heaven: a time to be born, and a time to die" (Eccles. 3:1–2, KJV). This ancient writer of the scriptures tells us what we all know intellectually: our earthly journey cannot last forever. But emotionally most of us are not prepared for the road to end—not for ourselves and not for loved ones. What makes the letting go easier for us as Christians is the truth that Jesus came to teach us: that the end of this life marks the beginning of a new one. The journey into death that each of us will one day take leads not into oblivion but into new life and the fullness of knowledge and truth.

6

Prayer and Healing

Eleanor and I have had a long-standing interest in prayer and healing. This interest intensified through our association with a nursing school at a community college when we lived in Florida. Our interest was also stimulated by colleagues who worked in medical professions. A concern these colleagues voiced was that hospitals—as well as their own professions—had what they considered restrictive policies about prayer, policies that limited them in their efforts to give patients emotional comfort.

The situation hasn't changed a lot over the years. I was recently made aware of this while working with a seminarian in a clinical pastoral education program at a Christian hospital. The student told how she had suggested to a family that they use the breath prayer as a way of focusing on God's presence. In the weekly conference with her supervisor, she was severely reprimanded for what she had done and warned not to try something like that again.

I want to make it clear that *I am steadfastly against imposing religion on anyone.* Never do I feel more strongly about this issue than when working with the dying. People are particularly vulnerable at this time and willing to grasp at anything if there is the slightest possibility it will help. Yet if we are to truly respond to the needs of patients and their families, there must be something more the clergy and other spiritual caregivers can do than say a perfunctory prayer at the end of a visit. And if there is a laying on of hands, we can do better than perform it in a ritualistic this-is-something-I'm-supposed-to-do fashion.

Adding the Emotional and Spiritual Dimension

Several years ago I was on an all-male hospice panel that included Baptist, Episcopal, Jewish, and Roman Catholic clergy. Before our discussion the coordinator solemnly said, "You know, gentlemen, we must be very careful when we talk about prayer. Our volunteers are not trained in that area, and we don't want them going in and praying with people. The purpose here today is simply to share what comes out of your experience."

How preposterous! There we were—a gathering of clergy—being told that the thing we were not supposed to share was our experience with prayer, which for me and perhaps the others was the most significant part of our ministry.

Some time later, I taught a course called "Prayer and Healing for the Health Professional." There was a lot of discussion about how much could be communicated through touch: stroking an arm, giving a gentle massage, holding a hand. I talked about ways the caregiver could pray and share in the laying on of hands without being obvious about it. People who took the course were very receptive. They hadn't been satisfied with just fulfilling the basic requirements of their jobs; they wanted to bring a dimension of spiritual and emotional nurturing to their work.

Although Claudia hadn't taken my course on prayer and healing, she was one of those health care professionals who felt that patients often had needs that weren't being met. I got to know Claudia because she was Frank's nurse. Frank was a husband, father, and member of my congregation. One day as he lay in the hospital near death, I stopped at the nurses' station to talk to Claudia. I explained that Frank was using a little prayer to help him focus his thoughts and be attentive to God's presence. "When Frank gets restless—or if it appears he's dying and family members aren't around—would you consider saying the prayer with him?" I asked. "I don't know if you'd feel comfortable doing this, but I'm certain Frank would appreciate it and so would his family."

Claudia looked at me with widened eyes. "I've been a nurse for five years," she said, "and this is the very first time any minister has ever talked to me about praying with a patient. I'm a Christian, and so often I've wanted to share scripture or a prayer but just stood by feeling helpless. I've seen that little prayer of Frank's by his bedside, and I certainly will use it. I wish I'd known about it last night when he was feeling so restless."

Carl and No Code

One day on a visit to Carl, I found him so dejected that he didn't even raise his eyes when I entered the room.

"Is your pain rough today?" I asked.

"Not the physical pain," he replied.

I had ceased being surprised by Carl's responses and the mature insights they often revealed. "Want to tell me what's happened?"

"Today I overheard someone outside my room say, 'Oh, my, he's so young. He didn't get a chance to live a full life.' " Carl spoke in a mocking voice and then asked angrily, "What the hell do they think I've been? Only half alive? To me, living a full life means using the time you've got to the fullest. I've done that, which is more than I can say for a lot of people who've already lived a lot longer than I'm going to. Why can't people stop seeing the world just from their point of view?"

For me, Carl's comments underscored how important it is when working with the dying to put aside our own point of view and try to see the world from theirs. This is best accomplished by being sensitive to their situation and by being a good listener; to have an antenna tuned to moods and feelings and hear what is said as well as not said.

Within a couple weeks of his remarks about a full life, Carl—the handsome young man who had once been a champion wrestler—was on No Code. That is, if he went into an acute, life-threatening state, no emergency action would be taken. Carl's illness had been prolonged and arduous, and this decision was one that he, along with his doctor and family, had made.

With Carl on No Code, I felt it was important for the nurses on all the shifts to know they could do something for him if a crisis arose and his family wasn't there. I told them about his prayer "Lead me to the light, O Lord," which they would find on a card beside his bed. It was, I explained, a prayer that he had been saying for a long time and one that captured his feeling about death: the Lord was going to lead him into the light. I suggested that after they had made him as comfortable as possible, they begin to say his prayer. "Keep saying it over and over," I said. "Even if Carl's not able to speak the words aloud, he'll be doing it in his mind and heart."

A motherly nurse named Beverly was especially affected by what I shared. Tears came to her eyes, and she said, "You have no idea what it's like to just stand by and watch the person on No Code die. What a relief it is to know that there's something I can do for Carl. Thank you so much."

Negatives with Religion

I don't want to give the impression that all religion—or at least what passes for religion—in the hospital setting is good. Quite the contrary. There have been, and continue to be, abuses in the name of religion, and they need to be addressed.

When I think of negative religious experiences, an incident with Carl comes to mind. One day when I came for a visit, I almost got run over by a portly man striding out of

Carl's room with a Bible under his arm. My clericals made it obvious that I was a minister, and the man stopped just long enough to shake his head and say with pity, "The poor kid's dying and still not ready to confess his sins and be saved."

Was this man really saying that Carl—who could have given all of us lessons in prayer and faith—was not going to know the glory of risen life unless he did things a certain, prescribed way? Unless he did them *this* man's way? That position was too absurd to dignify with a response.

It was obvious when I entered Carl's room that he had overheard what the man said to me. I walked over to the bed and gave him a hug. "I'm sorry about that, Carl. Want to talk about what went on with him?"

Carl shook his head in disbelief. "What a trip. He came in all smiles and introduced himself. Then he said he just wanted to read me some scripture. From the book in the Bible that he picked, I could tell what was coming: something about Jesus bringing fire and separating the good from the bad. I got scared, but then I remembered a tip you'd given me." He paused, and a small smile crept onto his face. "Remember when you told me that if visitors got to be too much, I should close my eyes and say my prayer? I did that, and I guess he thought I'd fallen asleep because he left!" (The advice I gave to Carl is what I tell all the seriously ill people I work with. Too often they wear themselves out trying to stay alert and end up ministering to the visitors!) A bit wistfully, Carl added, "Actually, I felt kind of sorry for him. He was trying so hard."

That statement was typical of Carl's maturity and his tolerance toward those who were in a different place spiritually. This had not been the only time someone approached Carl offering spiritual intercession that he rejected.

Earlier a woman from Carl's church brought what she

considered to be very exciting news. Jane, a member of the prayer group, had received word from God that Carl was going to be completely healed. The bearer of the news had expected Carl to be elated when, in fact, his reaction was quite the opposite. Jane's message came at a time when Carl not only accepted that he was going to die but was in so much pain he actually looked forward to death.

After Carl told me about the incident, I asked, "How would you feel if you were suddenly healed physically?"

"I don't want to be physically healed." His voice rose to a near shout. "I'm ready to die. That's what I've been preparing for!"

Carl died later that month, and Jane was devastated. Every aspect of her relationship with God came into question. She had told many people that a healing was to occur, and now she found it difficult even to go to her church.

Jane came to me for counseling about a year later. One of the discoveries she made was that ten years earlier she had denied her father's illness and never dealt with the anger she experienced when he died. In Jane's thinking, a healing for Carl would have somehow redeemed her own father's suffering and death. When she understood that, she felt more at peace with herself and her God.

The Power of Prayer

Many of us have heard of, and some of us have experienced, faith healings. Doctors acknowledge that there are instances in which terminally ill patients are restored to health and they can give no medical explanation for the recoveries.

There is much to be said for "claiming the healing" and praying for restored health. Indeed, there is power in prayer. Scripture tells us "the prayer of faith will save the sick" (James 5:15). Yet all of us can doubtless recall times—many times—when we have prayed for a healing and it did not occur. Does that mean that God was not listening? that our faith was too weak? or that our prayers were not fervent enough? I think not, but I also think it's fruitless to try to find an answer to why some people are healed and some are not.

Much of what happens on our earthly journey will remain a mystery until we get to our risen life. As the apostle Paul tells us, "Now we see through a glass, darkly; but then face to face: now I know in part; but then shall I know even as also I am known" (1 Cor. 13:12, KJV).

When we don't get the answer to prayer that we had hoped for—when a healing doesn't occur despite our earnest pleas—can we honestly say that our prayers were wasted? that we might as well not have prayed? I do not believe we can ever say prayer is wasted; some good always comes of it. Although our prayers may not change a situation and give us the miracle we want, *prayer changes us.* Through prayer, we find inner resources of strength and hope and courage we didn't know we had. Through prayer, we are no longer facing our fears and pain alone; God is there beside us, renewing our spirit, restoring our soul, and helping us carry the burden when it becomes too heavy for us to bear.

Another important value of prayer is the power it has to unite us. Time and time again I have seen relatives, friends, neighbors, and even strangers join in praying for someone who is ill, and for that person's family. Repeatedly, I have witnessed people of all faiths putting aside their theological differences and raising their minds and hearts to God on behalf of someone who has been the victim of an accident or illness. When we pray in such instances, we are in effect saying, "I'm hurting with you." One of the marvels of prayer is that distance poses no barrier. Wherever we are we can unite with others in an expression of loving concern through our prayers.

Cosmic Prayer

There are always those times when someone will ask, "Why does there need to be such pain?" "Why don't I just die and be relieved of this torment?"

These are real and hard questions for which I have only one response: "I don't know." But then I go on to say, "I'd like to share with you something that many people have found helpful to them in their pain. The apostle Paul tells us if we die with Jesus, we share in his resurrection as well.

"Jesus had his pain, you have yours, and a great many other people in the world have theirs. When pain gets bad, try being attentive to your breath prayer. Think—as you pray—of others in pain and unite your pain with theirs."

It is especially helpful if the person has someone specific in mind. People who live with illness usually know others who are also suffering. If they don't, I suggest the name of someone I know or ask them to remember victims of war, famine, or disasters such as hurricanes or earthquakes. Thinking of another hurting person makes pain and misfortune concrete and reminds the ill that they are not alone in their suffering. It is shared by many. I call the uniting of ourselves with the pain of others cosmic prayer.

The sick and dying who have prayerfully united themselves with the suffering of others tell me that it does not necessarily take away their pain, but it does change their attitude toward it. By reminding themselves that others are also suffering, they are better able to tolerate their situation. Through their pain and their prayer, they unite themselves with suffering humanity throughout the world and are more aware of their share in the redemption of Jesus.

7
The Gift of Touch

I'm not sure if I can handle this, I thought as I pulled open the door of the sturdy old brick building and stepped inside. I was newly ordained and this was my first visit to a parishioner in a nursing home. The last time I had been in such a place was on visits to my grandfather in the final years of his life. I again found myself in the same institutional setting, smelling disinfectant mingled with stale cooking odors and sensing the heaviness of time as people waited out their days. What would I do on this visit? What would I say? Should I be outgoing or solemn? Should I touch or not touch?

Since then I have become more comfortable on my visits to nursing homes. Such visits are, in fact, a particularly satisfying part of my ministry. As I look back on that early experience, I see that what I feared the most was physically touching the people. I had no feeling of connectedness; it was a "them and me" situation.

Today I just returned from the Trussville Health Care Center, our local health care facility (formerly called a nursing home). While there, I shared in the worship service and preached, something I do on a rotation basis with other ministers in the community. My involvement began some six years ago when I first arrived in Trussville. Bob Robinson, a layman in his seventies, views the facility as his special ministry and asked, a month in advance, if I would preach for them on a Wednesday morning. Because it was part of our church's outreach, I agreed. But again I was plagued with anxieties about what to say and do.

Bob welcomed me as I arrived that first Wednesday. "After you're finished, we'll sing," he explained. "Then it would be great if you could go around and greet each person. The residents love to have someone come in who reaches out and touches them."

There it was again: that matter of touching!

I still recall the first day with great clarity. The service began with a volunteer from one of the churches playing hymns on the piano. As I joined in the singing, I glanced around at the wheelchairs. With the exception of two men, all the chairs were occupied by women. Several of the patients were palsied, and some were supported in their chairs with cloth ties. A few were dozing off. Visitors were clustered in the back of the small chapel. I was to learn later that some of the visitors had a family member living at the center, and every Wednesday they came to visit and take part in the service. Other visitors saw it as their ministry to share time with the residents.

The hymn singing was followed by prayers for individuals. The list seemed to go on endlessly. Then came a devotional message given by another volunteer. Over the years, I continue to be impressed by the dedication and dependability of the many volunteers who so generously give of their time and talent.

After the devotional, it was my turn. Bob introduced me as the new minister in town, and I got up to preach. I remember enjoying it because I love to preach, and I certainly had a captive audience. Bob thanked me after I finished and then announced that we would sing hymn number thirty-eight. I was so preoccupied thinking about the logistics of moving among wheelchairs *and touching* everyone that I didn't even open the hymnal. The music began. I stepped forward, hesitant and unsure of myself. I reached for a gnarled hand here, touched an arm or shoulder there, sometimes waking the person up. I was halfway around the room before I really heard the hymn that was

being sung: "He Touched Me." In that instant I felt en-
folded in God's grace and tears welled up in my eyes. In
touching I was being touched.

After the service, I mentioned to Bob how affected I was
by hearing one of my favorite hymns. "He Touched Me"
became my theme song; throughout the years I have been
going to the center, Bob has seen to it that the hymn is
always sung at the end of the Wednesday worship service I
take part in. No matter how harried I may feel about
working the commitment into my schedule, I invariably
come away from the visit feeling touched in heart and
spirit.

Touching and Being in Touch

Touch is a gift we can give, one to another. No matter
what our age, most of us never lose our need to touch and
be touched. Psychologists refer to our need for touch as
"skin hunger." The sick and the dying have a particular
yearning for the emotional nurturing that comes from
gentle, caring touch.

Only a few illnesses prohibit us from touching patients.
Some people have skin sensitivity that makes touch painful, but here, too, the cases are rare. In situations where
the environment has to be kept sterile, we may have to put
on a gown and gloves. Even then we can still stroke an arm
or squeeze a hand. Sometimes I think we wish patients
were untouchable because we find it so difficult to touch
them.

Not long ago I was making a hospital visit to Nathan, a
cancer patient in his early forties. The doctor came in
while I was there. He said his stay would be brief, and it
wasn't necessary for me to leave. I moved to a corner of the
room to be as unobtrusive as possible and observed the
visit. At no time did the doctor reach out to Nathan with a
handshake or an encouraging pat on the shoulder. He did

not even get close enough to touch Nathan's bed. Just before leaving, he took a backward step and, tucking his chart under his arm, said, "Is there anything you want to ask me?"

"No, thank you, doctor," Nathan replied in a voice as lifeless as that doctor's visit.

Obviously there had been no physical touching in this instance, but had there been *any* kind of touching? *any* meeting of mind or heart that might in some way have nurtured Nathan? I did not see that there had been and was reminded of times in my ministry when, because I felt too busy or was distracted by other matters, I had done the same thing. An incident at Sarasota Memorial in Florida will always be a reminder to me that it is one thing to pay a visit to a patient and it is quite another to really be present and in touch with that person.

My destination was a room in the cardiac section, and I had to take a roundabout way to get there because the hospital was being remodeled. I entered the double room and found Harold in the bed by the window. He appeared tired, and his eyes had the lusterless look of someone in pain. I was uncomfortable being there and told myself I shouldn't stay very long. Besides, I had to see a lot of other patients that morning.

Harold looked up at me. "Please sit down, Father."

Ignoring his invitation, I said, "You don't need someone visiting for very long today, Harold."

"Yes, I do," he replied firmly. "*Please* sit down."

I felt as if a giant hand were pressing me into the chair while within me a voice said, "Right now, Harold is the only person in the world for you, *so sit!*" I eased into the chair and became attentive to my own breath prayer. It's something I do instinctively when I feel a particular need for the presence and guidance of God. Since that visit with Harold, I have always tried to let whomever I'm with be the most important person in the world to me at the moment. That, I think, is being in touch at a basic level. When we make ourselves present to someone else, we form a unique bond of caring, a bond wherein we feel the presence of God.

The Touch-Me-Nots

I have discovered that although most people need and like to be touched, some individuals do not want our touch. When we encounter such people, it is important to respect their physical space and be cautious about entering it. There are times when I feel the moment is right and push through the barrier of touch to attempt a warm, human connection. There are other times, however, when I feel it's best to do no more than touch the edge of the bed or rest my hands on the bed or bedside table. Sometimes I sit at the side of the bed and place the Bible or prayer book on it. There are no guidelines to follow in this matter; how to proceed rests with our intuition and clues we pick up from the individual's body language.

Those of us who go to a patient with the intention of prayer have an advantage over other visitors. Even the most ardent touch-me-not doesn't flinch too visibly when I extend my hand and ask, "Can we pray together?" When family and friends are present, I invite them to form a circle around the bed and join hands in prayer. There can be moments of awkwardness—especially if some of the visitors aren't praying people—but I have found those few awkward moments to be far outweighed by the good experiences. I can't count the number of times people have come to me afterward and said how meaningful the prayer circle was for them.

I believe that many touch-me-nots have the desire to touch and be touched. The trouble is, they don't know how to go about doing it. Although I don't believe in forcing touch on anyone, I have found that by taking the risk of reaching out, people usually respond in kind. Sometimes a warm embrace or a lingering clasp of the hand speaks more deeply of God's love and grace than words possibly could. Indeed, touch can create an environment wherein sharing and trust take root.

Creative Ways of Being in Touch

Even a patient's main caregiver cannot always be physically in touch, but there are other ways to be in contact—ways that touch the mind and heart. Of course phone calls and letters are the old standbys and, because they communicate so effectively, will always be popular. Our electronic age offers us many innovative means of being in touch with those confined to hospitals, nursing facilities, or their own homes.

I am continually amazed and delighted at the ways I see the bedridden using electronic equipment. Once when I entered the quiet of a hospital room where draperies were drawn to subdue the light, I was momentarily taken aback. There in bed lay thin, bald eighty-six-year-old Phillip recuperating from a hip replacement. Sitting beside the bed was his wife, Margaret. Both were wearing earphones connected to a portable stereo on the windowsill. When Margaret glanced up from the afghan she was knitting and noticed me, she gave a startled little jump and touched Phillip's arm. He turned off the stereo, and they removed the earphones, laughing as they eyed me.

"We couldn't stand a day without our music time," Margaret said. Then she told how at home they regularly listened to music in the evening. One of their sons knew they were spending a lot of time together in the hospital and sent them the stereo with two earphones.

"At first we felt a little silly putting those contraptions on our heads," Phillip said. "But listening to music has helped pass the time. Now all the nurses on the floor are

talking about the 'teenagers' listening to their 'box.' "
Bringing the familiar to the sick and dying is a
thoughtful and creative way of being in touch. People who
enjoy reading but are no longer able to read enjoy talking
books. Even people who can still read but are weakened by
illness often prefer to listen to books rather than read
them. Most bookstores and libraries have a wide variety of
books on tape, and more are becoming available.

When an elderly university professor who was an Eliz-
abethan scholar lay dying in the hospital, some of his
colleagues read to him from his favorite books. Word
spread and soon more faculty friends and former students
signed up as volunteers to read from a list of selections the
professor drew up. At first the professor objected to the
attention, saying he was putting people to too much trouble. In time, though, he stopped protesting because he
understood that this was the one way people could show
their appreciation for him. A former student who lived in
another part of the country heard about the project and
taped some favorite selections so the professor would have
something to listen to when no one was there to read to
him in person.

Hospital stays for young children can be frightening.
They feel out of touch with their families and sometimes
even abandoned. A good way to help a child feel a mother's
or a father's presence when neither can be there is to tape
some of the child's favorite stories. A story told in the
parent's familiar voice is especially comforting at bed-
time. Another way to keep a child in touch with the
familiar is to have classmates, neighbors, and relatives
tape words of friendly greeting and encouragement.

Ministry for the Church
Making tapes for shut-ins and the hospitalized is an
important ministry for the church. Parishioners can tape

readings from the Bible, prayers, or any material that uplifts and comforts. Cassette recordings can be made of the worship service, Bible classes, or other study groups. This has proven to be an effective way of keeping ill parishioners in touch with the church community. For the beginning volunteer, delivering the tapes and picking them up provide a good introduction to working with shut-ins and the hospitalized. For new volunteers who are ill at ease, the tapes are a springboard for conversation.

Touch and Ritual

Rituals have emerged throughout history as structured ways of touching during times of celebration and times of crisis. We use both signs and words in rituals to convey spiritual blessings. I find rituals helpful in creating a bond between myself and the seriously ill or dying person. Whether you are ordained or not, as a major caregiver you can share in rituals that usually are reserved for clergy.

Often when I visit a patient, I begin the conversation by saying, "Let's pray that God be with us in our visit and continue to grant you peace and wholeness." Or if there is a lull in the middle of my visit, I might say, "Let's take a moment and pray, thanking God that we can be together and that you are in God's care, (*person's name*)."

At the end of my visit, I say words to the effect of, "What a joy to be with you today. Let's give thanks for our time together and pray for continued blessings." I then place my hands over the person's head, being careful not to touch someone who does not want to be touched but close enough to give a feeling of connectedness. Or I may hold one hand in mine and put my other hand on the patient's shoulder or forehead. If appropriate, I place both my hands over the diseased area.

Sometimes I pray a spontaneous prayer; at other times I use a formal prayer that I have memorized, or I simply recite the Lord's Prayer. If the person is using a breath prayer, I often suggest we use that. I end my prayer by making a sign of the cross on the person's forehead and bless in the name of the Father, Son, and Holy Spirit. Otherwise I say, "Remember, (*name*), that in baptism you were signed as Christ's own forever"; or "Remember, (*name*), that you are saved through the cross and resurrection of Jesus."

The Use of Oil in Ritual

There are references in the Old and New Testaments to oil being used in ritual. Take, for example, this passage regarding the use of oil for healing: "Is any among you sick? Let him call for the elders of the church, and let them pray over him, anointing him with oil in the name of the Lord" (James 5:14). James seems to assume that the practice was well-known among the readers of his letter.

Some Christian denominations still use oil in rituals. That is the case in the Episcopal tradition. On Maundy Thursday, our bishop calls for all the ordained to celebrate the remembrance of the Lord's Supper and to renew our ordination vows. At the ceremony, he also blesses the oil we will be using in our healing ministry.

I keep my oil in a small vial filled with cotton. In the ritual that is commonly called the Anointing of the Sick, I dab my thumb in the oil and make the sign of the cross on the patient's forehead. While making the sign, I sometimes say, "I anoint you with the oil of healing and gladness in the name of the Father, and of the Son, and of the Holy Spirit (or . . . in the name of Jesus, the Healer)."

Other times I use this formal prayer:

As you are outwardly anointed with this holy oil, so may our heavenly Father grant you the inward anointing of the Holy Spirit. Of his great mercy, may he forgive you your sins, release

you from suffering, and restore you to wholeness and strength. May he deliver you from all evil, preserve you in all goodness, and bring you to everlasting life; through Jesus Christ our Lord. Amen.
                              —The Book of Common Prayer

Some people, particularly those from a Roman Catholic background, might regard the anointing I have just described as the Last Rites or sacrament of Extreme Unction (Latin for "last anointing"). Until about twenty years ago, the anointing took place only when a person was believed to be dying. Although the sacrament is now called the Anointing of the Sick, many who grew up in that older Catholic tradition still think the anointing is done only at life's end. I was made aware of this when I mentioned to a woman who had grown up in the Roman Catholic faith that I wanted to share the oil of healing with her. She recoiled, eyes wide as she asked, "I'm not dying, am I?" I quickly assured her that she was not.

Giving Permission to Die
    "Ron, I've got a problem and I think you can help," said the voice on the phone. The caller was a Baptist pastor and a friend whose church was across town. "A member of my congregation has been dying for the last four days, but keeps hanging on," he explained. "The man's wife just called and said, 'Please come and do something to let Jake know that it's okay to die. He needs someone to give him permission.' "
    My pastor friend went on to say that he had attended a workshop in which I told a story about anointing someone just before death. "Can you tell me where I can get some oil?" he asked. "And then brief me on what to do?"
    I offered him some of my blessed oil, but felt he should know about the alternative of using olive oil that he blessed himself. "This oil doesn't have to be anything

special," I said. "Whatever you can buy in the grocery store will do. You can bless it by saying a simple prayer such as, 'God, I ask you to make this holy oil that it may be a source of grace and blessing.' "

Perhaps you prefer a more formal prayer such as this one:

> *O Lord, holy Father, giver of health and salvation: Send your Holy Spirit to sanctify this oil; that, as your holy apostles anointed many that were sick and healed them, so may those who in faith and repentance receive this holy unction be made whole; through Jesus Christ our Lord, who lives and reigns with you and the Holy Spirit, one God, for ever and ever. Amen.*
> —**The Book of Common Prayer**

Sam's Ritual of Good-bye

Sam was a kindly husband and father who kept slipping in and out of consciousness but was lucid during his awake moments and knew he was dying. The family had gathered around his bed, and we all joined in celebrating the Eucharist. Sam was too ill to swallow, so I dipped my finger in the chalice and placed some wine on his lips. Even though this happened quite some time ago, I'm still moved each time I recall Sam licking his lips to receive communion.

After we finished with communion, I explained to the family that our Christian heritage includes a special service for anointing the dying. "There are times of sorrow when words fail us," I said. "Then it's helpful to share in a ritual that helps us say good-bye."

The family members agreed they would like this for Sam, and for themselves. I asked that everyone gather close around the bed. Then I said a prayer of thanks for Sam's life; for the years he had spent among us; for his love for and devotion to his family. Next I took out my blessed oil and began a ritual I have found meaningful. It involves making the sign of the cross on each of several parts of the body while saying a brief prayer I have composed. You may want to sbustitute prayers of your own:

On the forehead: "May your mind, which has served you well here in this life, now be conformed more and more to the mind of Christ, that you may know God."

On the eyes: "May your eyes now see the glory that has been prepared for those who love God."

On the ears: "May the sound of Jesus calling your name bring comfort and joy to you."

On the mouth: "May the words of your mouth become praise with the angels and hosts of heaven as you proclaim that Jesus is Lord."

On the hands: "May your hands be lifted in praise and open to the embrace of Jesus."

On the feet: "May you walk with Jesus into a place of peace and rest."

On the heart: "May your heart be so filled with grace and love that you enter peacefully into the heart of God."

Then I asked all who had gathered in the circle to extend their hands and touch Sam: "And now, Sam, we commend you to God's care, to enter into that which has been prepared for you." To conclude, we all joined in saying the Lord's Prayer.

This kind of ritual at life's end brings the family great comfort and relief. It's a way to say good-bye, and at the same time gives family members the feeling they have helped their loved one make the passage from this life to the next. For the person who is dying, the ritual gives permission to let go of the familiar and enter the unknown.

Each time I am a part of helping someone cross over to

the next life, I take particular meaning from a passage in one of Paul's letters:

> *Therefore, since we are surrounded by so great a cloud of witnesses, let us also lay aside every weight, and sin which clings so closely, and let us run with perseverance the race that is set before us, looking to Jesus the pioneer and perfecter of our faith, who for the joy that was set before him endured the cross, despising the shame, and is seated at the right hand of the throne of God.*
>
> **—Hebrews 12:1–2**

For Sam, it turned out that our ritual came within hours of the end of his race. His family and I had been part of that great "cloud of witnesses" who encouraged him on to victory.

8
The Breath Prayer
Opens Other Doors

Fred was known in his community as a generous person, the sort of man we think of as a kindly grandfather—patient, wise, interested in others. Now he was terminally ill and bedridden. He shared his breath prayer with me and then surprised me by asking that I share mine with him. I was touched as he said, "I'd like to be able to pray with you as well as having you pray with me." It was a wonderfully thoughtful thing for him to think of, yet I hesitated. My prayer was too personal. Too private. Too much a part of me.

Suddenly I was ill at ease. Knowing Fred's prayer and the prayers of others I worked with seemed "in the line of duty." It was part of my job, and if people wished it, I shared their prayers with family, friends, and nursing staff. Now Fred was looking at me, waiting for my response. Reluctantly I said, "My prayer is 'Father, let me feel your presence.' " In that moment of sharing, I felt an even deeper sense of identification with Fred and a strengthening of the bond that already existed between us.

Trust begins to build whenever we pray with others. We feel a kind of spiritual partnership wherein we admit our fears, reveal our hopes, acknowledge our sorrows. This is particularly true when someone shares the breath prayer. Because it is so spiritually self-revealing, the person doing the sharing has to have a high degree of trust. Where such trust exists, doors open to many areas of the patient's life, and we become deeply involved in the person's process of living and dying.

The Life Review

On one of my visits to Emily, an elderly stroke victim who had been spry all her life but was now bedridden, she confided, "I get so frustrated! I can remember the layout of my grandmother's house and conversations I had with her, but I can't remember what I did yesterday or whether I'm repeating myself in a conversation."

Although Emily's experiences with memory are typical of stroke victims, I find that among the elderly in general, vivid recall of the past is common. So often they want to tell their stories. At one time I thought this was merely conversation that extended a visitor's stay, but I've come to realize that much more is involved. In retelling stories, people affirm who they are in their own eyes as well as in the eyes of God. I now encourage people I counsel and console to do a life review.

A life review is exactly that: a review of one's life. We have all heard of—and perhaps some of us have experienced—an instantaneous life review when, in a near-death situation, portions of our life appeared like flashbacks in a movie. The kind of review I'm suggesting is like that only done in an unhurried, reflective manner. This is important for the elderly, and especially for those in the dying process, because it helps them move more gently from this life to the next.

A review of the past is a way for people to bring their lives up to date. As they reflect on those who shaped their lives and the events that brought them both sadness and joy, the years come into perspective. Out of a life review come stories that are part of a family's heritage. But in our mobile society, relatives often are not around to hear the oral history that deserves to be passed from one generation to another. Personal histories will be lost in many families if the elderly do not have some means of passing them on.

When Emily commented that she could remember the past but not the present, I said, "Since you can recall what happened long ago in such detail, why don't we create something to pass on to your children and grandchildren? We could call it 'This Is Your Life.' "

Emily looked puzzled. "What do you mean?"

"Do you have any pictures?"

"Do I have pictures!" Emily rolled her eyes as though suggesting I had no idea what I was getting into. "I have boxes of pictures and even whole drawers full of them."

"Good. Then that's where we'll begin." And begin we did. Because of the severity of the stroke, Emily was confined to her bed. She told me where the pictures could be found, and I gathered them all in one place. With the help of some teen and adult volunteers, we went through the photos. We asked Emily about names and dates and marked them on the backs. (We used a soft lead pencil to prevent possible damage to prints anyone might one day want to have copied.) Some of the photos called forth stories, but none of Emily's family lived nearby to hear them, so volunteers either taped them or wrote them out in longhand. Eventually the photos and their accompanying stories were passed on to family members.

Special Stories

Another way to help people get into a life review is to ask if there are stories they would like to share with members of their family—children, grandchildren, nieces, nephews. I remember Harold telling me about his grandson's graduation and subsequent vacation at a summer camp. He then said, "You know when I was his age, I did something similar."

"Have you ever told your grandson about that?" I asked.

Harold shrugged off the question. "Nah, he wouldn't be interested."

"Let's try anyway," I urged. "Why don't we put the story on a cassette tape so you can send it to him as a belated graduation gift?" As you might have guessed, the grandson appreciated the tape. The younger grandchildren who heard about it besieged Granpop Harold with requests to tape special stories for them, too.

Tales of Ketchup and Pajamas

The idea of a life review took root in our family several years ago. My then seventy-four-year-old father was talking with our young son and daughter when something in their conversation caused him to tell about the first time he saw ketchup and pajamas. Paul and Anne thought the story was hilarious and wanted to hear more about the *old,* olden days. (Eleanor and I lived in the *olden* days!) At the children's urging, Grandpa retold the story to the delight of the rest of the family. That was when I suggested he find a way to record the stories. At first Dad resisted, but I kept pushing. My most persuasive argument was that if he didn't do it, his stories would largely be forgotten and his descendants the poorer for never having known them.

Eventually he picked up on the suggestion. As of this writing, he has filled twelve cassette tapes and isn't finished yet. In doing his life review, he has gained insights into past events and relationships, relived happy occasions, and engaged in a number of nostalgic conversations with brothers and sisters about things he couldn't fully remember. My mother is now involved in recording some of her stories in a memory book. Of course the greatest benefit of their life reviews will be to us, their family. When my parents are no longer here to tell us about the past, we will have their tapes and writings to help us remember them and what they stood for.

Letters of Farewell

David was dying, and although his family made frequent visits, his lingering illness made it impossible for them to be with him all the time. He reached a point where he was unable to move and could speak only in a whisper. I asked if he would like to leave any messages for his family. "I'd be glad to write each of them a letter that you dictate and then make certain they get them after your death," I offered. "That would be a beautiful gift to leave them."

David motioned for me to come closer. When I did, he whispered, "I'd like that very much." So we began, starting with his eldest child and going through the family. Some of the letters were short, containing just a loving thought. Others were longer, recounting a fondly recalled incident.

When David died, I preached at his funeral as he had suggested. I talked about our legacy living on and how, as David neared the end of his life, he wrote letters to his children and grandchildren. There were many tears that day, especially among those who were moved by the realization that David had been thinking of them during those final days.

The family gathered at David's home after the service, and I handed out the letters. A sacred silence touched the room as family members read their personal messages. The quiet held until one of the younger grandchildren asked another, "What did Popo say to you?" The question created immediate interest in sharing the messages. The result was that each person read his or her letter aloud, right down to the young mother who read a note to her infant child from his grandfather.

Gifts of Remembrance

In an earlier chapter I talked about Mabel who had been systematically giving her possessions to relatives and friends. Each of her gifts was accompanied by a note telling why she had chosen a certain gift for a certain person.

Giving away possessions that have special meaning is a good way to ease into a life review. To be able to "tell a story" about a plate, a vase, a special shawl, or even tools from a workbench opens the doors to memories that turn small gifts into treasures. Mabel had been giving her possessions away over a period of years, but if time is limited, the gifts can be given all at once.

Gregory was a widower in his seventies with two sons, two daughters, and a large number of grandchildren. One day as I visited with him, he said, "It'll be hard for the kids to come and clean out my place. I hope they don't end up squabbling over my things."

It was the perfect opening to suggest that *he* decide what the various children and grandchildren should have. "Why not do some giving now?" I said. "There's more than one way to go about it. You can tell your children what you're doing, but let them wait to find out what they're getting until after you're gone. Another possibility is to give them the gifts now . . . or you might want to do some of both."

Gregory decided to write a letter to each child, stating what he was doing. Along with the letter, he sent a small gift chosen from among his possessions. He made it clear that he was making his decisions based on memories associated with the items, not on their monetary worth. He taped a note on each item to give its history and explain what it meant to him. Then together Gregory and I made a master list of what he wanted family members to have after his death. I remember one item on the list: a set of bookends his high-school history teacher had made and given to him when he went off to college. Gregory wanted them to go to one of his granddaughters who would be starting college in the fall.

A Swan Song for the Family

Patricia was a very proper, family-oriented matron who had never married. To relatives, she was the respected and beloved "Aunt Patricia." As I helped her plan her funeral, we talked about what hymns she wanted and discussed details about her burial. In jest I said, "What should I preach about, Patricia?"

She replied with a trace of humor, "I was just getting around to that!" She went on to say that she thought I should talk about what it's like never to have your own immediate family, but how there was something special about being the one who could always be confided in and who could give advice, then not have to live with it. She wanted the family to know how kind it was of them to include her in their lives and how much she appreciated the many good times they had given her.

Another of Patricia's requests was that following the funeral all the family gather for a good meal at her favorite small restaurant near the church. "I've got an idea, Patricia," I said. "Instead of my telling the family how you feel about them, why don't you do it yourself? We can make a tape, and I'll play it at the meal. It will be your swan song to the people who mean the most to you!"

Patricia liked the idea, and we set about doing it. This incident took place several years ago; had it occurred today, I would have suggested a videotape. The family would then have been left with both the sight and the sound of Patricia and no doubt viewed the tape at other gatherings where they felt the loss of her presence.

Setting Things Right

Joyful events are not the only things recalled in the life review process. Failures, disappointments, and old animosities are likely to surface as well. Often the dying want to apologize for wrongs in their past; this is especially true if they have hurt someone. They want to "clean the slate" in the time left to them and die with an untroubled conscience. But frequently when a spiritually troubling incident is brought up—particularly one that happened far in the past—family and even clergy dismiss it. "That's been forgiven long ago" is a stock response. "Why don't you just forget about it?"

If the wrong could have been easily forgotten, the person would have done so. The fact that it's brought up tells us it's a worrisome matter that needs to be addressed before the person can have peace of mind and heart. Instead of suggesting that the matter be forgotten, how much better to say, "Why don't you write or call the person? Say how you feel and ask for forgiveness."

Sometimes a wrong has been done by the person to someone who has died. We can then suggest that the individual tell the story to a member of the offended person's family and ask to be forgiven.

Imagery is also useful in helping people lay old hurts to rest. This is true whether people feel they have done something wrong or been wronged themselves. One way to lead people in healing imagery is to ask that they close their eyes and imagine the person they have wronged (or been wronged by) standing in front of them. Then tell them to talk to that person as if he or she were alive and real, venting their anger, resentment, hurt, or whatever their feelings may be. After people have talked themselves out, I ask that they forgive the person or seek forgiveness, depending on the circumstance. I also suggest that they see or sense Jesus there with his healing, loving power. This process often provides the assurance of forgiveness.

Some people find it easier to close their eyes and visualize the incident that distresses them. We can guide them in their imagery by saying, "Imagine that you are back (on the farm . . . in the old house . . . at the office). Standing right in front of you is (name). Look (name) in the eye and say, 'I forgive you for everything you did that hurt and angered me. I ask you to forgive me for whatever I did that hurt you.'"

It is a simple procedure, yet I have seen the immense relief that comes when people rid themselves of guilt and old hurts that have been weighing on them for years.

A Formal Ritual of Forgiveness

There are times when people need a formal ritual of forgiveness. This is especially true if they fear damnation for sins they have committed or for actions they consider to be sinful. Notice that I said *consider to be sinful.* Some people can be told over and over that something is not a sin, but if within their heart they think it is, no amount of talking will convince them otherwise. For such people, I recommend that they make a list of their sins, beginning with their most recent remembrance and then going back to remember as many sins as possible. After they have made their list, I suggest they read it privately to God and say a prayer asking for forgiveness. It can be a prayer said in their own words, or I may give them this prayer to say:

God of all creation, I ask pardon for my faults,
for all the times when I have said or thought or done
things harmful to myself or others.
I regret those times when through negligence
I did not do, think, or say what would have helped.
Forgive me as I forgive others who have harmed me.
I ask to be forgiven in Jesus' name.
Amen.

In some instances, I ask people if they would like to share their list with me so that I can give them the blessing of forgiveness. For members of denominations that do not have a tradition of private confession, simple prayers like the following bring comfort and peace:

Hear the good news:
"Christ died for us while we were yet sinners:

105

that proves God's love toward us."
In the name of Jesus Christ, you are forgiven!
—A Service of Word and Table

May Almighty God in mercy receive your confession of
sorrow and of faith, strengthen you in all goodness,
and by the power of the Holy Spirit
keep you in eternal life. Amen.
—The Book of Common Prayer

Friends: Believe the good news of the gospel.
In Jesus Christ, we are forgiven.
—The Worshipbook

While assisting the dying in seeking forgiveness, I often have the feeling that I am at a birthing. As layers of guilt and grievances are peeled back and reconciliations made, a new self emerges. It is a person who has looked into her soul or his soul with sincerity and honesty and laid the past to rest. Then with a sense of joy and anticipation, that person is free to move on.

9
Saying Good-bye

Stan's family was at that in-between place, wanting life to end, yet not wishing death on their husband and father. Stan was lying in the bedroom. His wife Maria, daughter Susan, son Mike, and I sat in the kitchen around the table in front of the window. We had sat together before, but this time was different. We knew the end was near.

Stan's prolonged suffering had already placed an incredible strain on the family's energy and emotions. Maria had lived with the daily stress of his illness for months. Susan was making visits that meant a 150-mile drive. Mike was taking time off work. We see in situations such as this how far the boundaries of love and duty can be stretched.

Those of us who work with the dying and their families find ourselves in a unique position. Although we are outsiders (that is, nonmembers of the family), our role as spiritual caregivers makes us insiders. Often family members become so numb with grief and strain that they look for leadership from someone who is outside yet close to the family.

As I sat at the table with Stan's family that morning, I knew this might be the last time the three of them would be together while Stan was still alive. Each of them needed to have a final word *alone* with him, yet at the same time feel the closeness of one another. "Friends," I began, "Stan is still conscious enough to know who you are, to hear you, and to talk to you. It's time to say your good-byes."

All eyes turned to me with the apprehensive look I had seen each time I led them a little farther along the road to

107

being survivors. "Oh!" was the only audible response I heard.

"I know it will be difficult," I said, "but we're here to support one another. What I suggest is that you begin, Maria. Then Susan because she's the oldest. After Susan speaks with her father, it will be Mike's turn."

Although their discomfort was apparent in the way they looked at one another, there was also the quiet and accepting sense that this was the time. The family turned to me for guidance on how to proceed. This is often the situation in times of personal crisis: people know they should do something but don't know just what that something is. Even when they do know, they are uncertain how to begin.

"When you go into Stan's room, I want you to do these four things," I told the family. Then I went through them step-by-step:

"First, hold his hand and recall a pleasant memory you have of him. If we think back, each of us has at least one special memory of a person we've been close to. Take a few moments to share that remembrance.

"Second, ask his forgiveness. You can do this by simply saying, 'Stan (or Dad), I ask you to forgive me for any harm or hurt I have caused you over the years.'

"Third, say, 'I forgive you for any harm or hurt that you caused me.'

"Then say your good-bye. Assure him that you want to be at his bedside when he dies, but in case you're not, you want to say your farewell now."

I looked from Maria to Susan to Mike. Their faces were solemn. "Each of you needs your private time with Stan," I said. "Give him the gift of completing all your business. And remember, it's a gift to you as well as to him."

At this point I wanted to leave, knowing that what I had proposed would be a highly emotional and intimate family happening. Yet I knew I needed to be there. Without my support and encouragement, they might not go through with it. "Maria, you go first," I said. "Remember: share a happy memory, ask his forgiveness, forgive him, and say good-bye. All the while you're gone, we'll be here praying for you."

In a short time, Maria came back to the kitchen with tears moistening her cheeks. Then Susan went to her father, and finally Mike, although hesitant, walked down the hall to the bedroom.

Mike seemed greatly relieved when he returned and talked about the memory he had shared with his father. Then they all discussed the experience and what it had meant to them.

Stan was still alive a week later, and I was once again visiting the family. Susan had again driven the 150 miles to be there for the weekend. She took me aside as I was about to leave. "Thank you for what you made us do the last time I was home. Before that, I was always afraid that when I left I'd never see Daddy alive again. It was something I'd worry about every day. This week for the first time, I wasn't worried at all because I'd said my good-bye. Even though I know he'll probably die while I'm away, that's okay now."

On my next visit, I, too, said my good-bye to Stan. I explained that I would be going out of town on a retreat and this might be our last time together. "I want to thank you for being so honest with me, and for being a friend," I said. "If this is our good-bye, then stay in peace."

About a month later, I was visiting with Maria and Susan who had come home for a few days. Mike was at work. The three of us visited for a while in the kitchen before I went to sit with Stan for a bit. When I walked into the bedroom, I found him dead. No one had been at his side, but we had all said our good-byes.

So often I have to sit with survivors after a death and listen to their remorse about unfinished business and not being there when a loved one died. Because it's often impossible for family members to be present at the time of death, it's important to have a ritual in which they can say their good-byes. That way they will always have something to remember as their final time together.

The Next Best Thing

When family members don't have the opportunity to say their good-byes, they can do the next best thing. My father-in-law died unexpectedly in his sleep, and his son who lived in the same city was called first. Tom went over immediately and later told the family that even though he knew his father was dead, he walked into the bedroom to say good-bye. He went on to say, "Since you couldn't be there, I also said good-bye to Dad for each of you." That small act was a grand one. It meant so much to all the children to know that in a sense they had said good-bye through Tom. There had been a final moment.

Forgiveness Is Difficult

As the story of Stan indicated, one of the aspects of saying good-bye is asking for and seeking forgiveness. Forgiveness is at the core of our Christian faith. In the prayer Jesus taught us, he said, "Forgive us our trespasses as we forgive those who trespass against us." Scripture contains many references to forgiveness. In one of the Gospels we are told, "If you forgive others the wrongs they have done to you, your Father in heaven will also forgive you" (Matt. 6:14-15, TEV).

Jesus is telling us that ours is a forgiving God, and as Christ's followers, we are called to share the gift of forgiveness. Although we should be doing our forgiving throughout our lifetime, it is certainly better to be reconciled with people in their final days than never to be reconciled at all.

I was made aware of just how important forgiveness is— and also how difficult it can be—during my mother-in-law's illness. She was on dialysis three days a week, and her condition was complicated by a bad heart. Our family had gone to St. Louis for a visit, realizing that this might be the last time we saw her alive. I knew that on this trip I *had* to do what I'd been putting off for a long time: I had to ask forgiveness for all the distress I had caused over our denominational parting of the ways.

I procrastinated until the last day of our visit. My mother-in-law and I were in the kitchen, just the two of us. It was the perfect time, but I kept stalling, trying to build up my courage. Just when the words were ready to come, someone walked in on us. *I was saved,* but only for a while. I would have to look for another opportunity to do what had to be done.

That opportunity didn't come until we were getting ready to leave. I was walking my mother-in-law down the hallway to the front door of her apartment building. This was my last chance. I took a deep breath, stopped in the middle of the hallway, and turned to face her. "Mom," I said, "I want to ask your forgiveness for all the hurt I've caused you over the years. I'm sorry that things haven't always been what you wanted." She just looked at me wordlessly. I don't know why she had no response and at the moment didn't care. I had done what I had to do, and I was free. Eleanor's mother lived for another year and a half, and I truly enjoyed our later visits, thanks in part to having taken care of my unfinished business with her.

Planning Is a Way to Say Good-bye

There are many ways to say good-bye, and not all of them should take place at the very end of one's life. Making plans for the inevitability of death is a forward-thinking and thoughtful way to say good-bye to people who will have to tend to matters after we are dead. This includes leaving a will, letting family members know where important documents can be found, and making funeral plans. My parents have always kept me informed about such matters. Each time they leave on a trip, they hand me an envelope that contains information and instructions I will need in the event of their deaths. They have even had a cemetery marker engraved with their names and put in place. Because I am their only surviving child, making final arrangements and settling their estate will be rather simple.

This kind of planning is one of the most caring things people can do for their survivors. Each family needs to find its own way of handling such matters.

Several years ago when Eleanor's parents were both alive, all the children had come to the family home in St. Louis for a reunion. We were gathered around the table for Sunday dinner, and at the end of the meal, Mom said, "With you all here, we want to do two things: we want to plan our funerals, and I want to start dividing up some of our possessions."

Suddenly the room fell quiet. But after the surprise of the announcement wore off, there was a warm discussion about how the service should be done, including readings to be read and songs to be sung. Both parents said that after their memorial service (they had willed their bodies to the medical school), they would like a reception in the church hall at which there would be sandwiches and punch. They asked that all the people who came to the reception be greeted personally and thanked for coming.

There was not a dry eye around the table that day the discussion took place. It was difficult at the time to think about endings, but as death took Eleanor's father and then her mother, the family was ever so grateful for the planning they had done. Family members were feeling scattered and didn't want to have to make decisions. What a blessing it was to simply get out the sheet of paper on which the parents' wishes had been written.

Churches Can Help

Some churches offer end-of-life planning as part of their adult enrichment program. These sessions cover such topics as the need for an updated will and the importance of having insurance papers and other key documents accessible. The sessions also urge people to make their own funeral plans and burial arrangements. For those who choose to do it, help is made available. I am always pleased by the many good ideas that come forth in these sessions and how freeing it is for people to be given permission to make such plans.

A church where I once served had a large number of retired parishioners. A form was drawn up that invited people to make suggestions about the kind of funeral they would like to have and to write down pertinent information for a newspaper obituary. We also asked that they list names, addresses, and phone numbers of their children. This was important because we had run into situations in which an elderly person died and we had no way of notifying the children who lived in other cities and states.

At some point, I try to ask all my elderly parishioners about the final arrangements they have made. Most often the matter comes up when we are talking about the death of a friend, when they are ill, or even when their activities are curtailed. After a funeral service for one of my parishioners, I talked to Sarah, who was in her sixties. She commented, "I'd never seen the Easter candle lighted at a funeral before. And what you said about death being the completion of baptism was lovely. I'd like to have the lighting of the candle at my funeral."

"Maybe we need to sit down and talk about that to be sure you get what you want," I said. "Have you made any of your wishes known to your family?"

Sarah took her head. "Every time I bring the matter up they pooh-pooh it."

"How about if I call you next week?" I suggested. "In the

meantime, give some thought to the kind of funeral you'd like to have, and we'll get some of your wishes down on paper."

When I met with Sarah, I learned that as she attended funerals over the years, she had been picking up ideas. "Every time one of my friends dies, I sit at the funeral and think, *This could be me,*" Sarah said. "So then my thoughts turn to what I'd like to have done when my time comes."

I assured Sarah that thinking about her own funeral was a good and natural thing to do; it showed that she accepted her mortality and saw death as a part of life. We had come to a point in our conversation when the time seemed right to bring up some matters relating to death. "By the way, Sarah," I said, "do you have your important papers in a place where your family will be able to get to them? I'm referring to such things as your will, insurance records, a list of your possessions, and how you want them distributed."

Sarah had her papers together, but it never occurred to her to let someone know where they could be found, nor had she given any thought to who would get her belongings. Following our conversation, Sarah again approached her children, and this time she would not be put off. Not only did they listen, but her sons—one age thirty-nine and the other forty-three—decided it was time to make their wills!

The Case for Getting Affairs in Order

In working with the dying, we can get into situations where there is a lot of family tension. It is often triggered by disagreements or uncertainties regarding wills, burial possibilities, and similar matters. In some cases, the dying person has left no will and made no mention about how possessions should be distributed. Although family members may know this should be taken care of, nobody wants to bring the matter up for fear of making it seem there is no longer any hope. On the other hand, there are cases in which the sick person wants to make arrangements, but thinks it will upset the family too much because no one wants to talk about death.

We need to get people past the idea that preplanning is morbid. Here again the church has a role to play. I ask couples who come to me for premarriage counseling if they have wills. Usually they laugh because they feel they won't have many possessions other than their wedding gifts and some hand-me-down furniture. Even so, I encourage them to make one out, particularly if either of the parties has an ex-spouse or children from another marriage.

In my travels when I have gone into dangerous areas, I have taken the time to write out some details about my possessions and suggestions for a funeral. Far from being morbid, it is enlivening to me. It helps me focus on the meaning my family has for me and my deep love for them. Sometimes I am able to say on paper what I am not able to express in person.

People who make known their wishes about their own funeral spare family members a great deal of decision-making at a time when they are least able to make good choices. If survivors have to make decisions about the casket, burial, flowers, music, and related matters, they tend to put their emotions on hold so they can be in control to take care of the tasks at hand. But somewhere down the road they have to express their sorrow. Unfortunately—when it is their time to grieve—they may have to do it alone because most of the other mourners will have returned to the routine of their lives. In situations where final arrangements have been made, the survivors are free to grieve while still surrounded by the comfort and support of a grieving community.

"Not in a Cigar Box!"

Sometimes my work with the dying involves my going to the funeral home with family members. It is important to visit the funeral home beforehand and find out what procedures are available and how matters are handled. Once when I had not done my homework, the family and I ended up being embarrassed.

George had been cremated, and I went with the family to pick up the cremains so we could bury them in a garden at the church. The family members were aghast when the funeral director brought them a cardboard container. George's wife burst into tears. "Not in a cigar box!" she cried. (Indeed, that's what the particular container looked like.) What a learning experience for me!

I discovered that the cremains can be received in several ways and I should have let the crematorium staff know that the family—and not a funeral director—would be picking them up. Now when someone wants some information about cremation, I am much better able to supply it.

It is a great help and comfort to the family if they go to the funeral home accompanied by someone who can offer suggestions. The presence of this objective adviser eases the pressure of decisions that have to be made. Money is frequently a very real concern. When this is the case, I try to keep costs down by asking the funeral director questions that don't occur to the family. For example, "It's important that we spend carefully, so would you please help us keep costs to a minimum?" "May we view caskets from just the middle to the lowest price range?" Or "Is the more expensive casket really that different from this one?"

Flowers are the traditional remembrance at funerals. Those who are having their first experience with the death of a loved one may need to be reminded that the family can request that money given in the deceased's name go to medical research, charities, scholarship funds, churches, and any number of other worthwhile organizations and causes. Such donations become a living memorial and lasting good-bye to the one who has died.

10
Making the Passage to Risen Life

Sylvia looked troubled as she came up to me after a Sunday Eucharist and asked if we could talk. "It's my Aunt Mary," she said. "You know, the one in the nursing home."

I nodded. "I visited your aunt the other day. She isn't as alert as she once was."

"Last night I had a call from the nursing home supervisor," Sylvia said anxiously. "She thinks Mary's going downhill fast; Mary's even telling the staff she wants to die. On my visits lately, she's been talking really strange. I don't know what to make of it . . . and it scares me." Sylvia fidgeted with the strap on her purse as though hesitant to continue.

"What does your aunt say?" I asked.

"Well . . . last night will give you some idea of why I'm so worried about her. She was very alert and seemed her usual self when I went into her room. She greeted me and then said, 'Did you see your Uncle Jack in the hallway? He just left. We had a wonderful visit, and he looks so good.'" Deep frown lines creased Sylvia's forehead as she confided, "I think she's losing her mind. Uncle Jack has been dead for years."

The experience was a familiar one, and I tried to calm Sylvia. "Your aunt isn't losing her mind," I said. "She's simply preparing to die. It's not uncommon for people moving closer to death to 'see' loved ones who've already passed on to risen life."

"Well, there's more!" Sylvia said confidentially. "The past couple of weeks she's been talking about other relatives who're *long* dead. She tells stories about them like they're still alive and relives entire conversations they have together. I don't know what to do. What can I say when she carries on like that?"

"Your aunt could be hallucinating," I said. "It's also possible that she's reacting to medication or even living in a pleasant dream world. Another possibility is that the deceased are actually coming to help her make the passage from this life . . . "

Sylvia looked at me with a stunned expression.

" . . . but the central issue is not whether the experiences are real or even why she's having them," I continued. "The important thing is that for her, things that may seem unreal to us are her reality. The best thing you can do is to act as if the people she speaks about are real to you, too. Encourage her to talk. And listen to her stories!"

Sylvia accepted that as something to consider. Then she told me more about her aunt. "Often she forgets she's in a nursing home and thinks she's back on the farm. Last night she said that Uncle Jack came to see her and said they were going to their new home soon. She couldn't understand that because the old house was just fine and asked me why they needed a new home."

"The next time you visit your aunt and she mentions her husband, tell her that one of these times he'll ask her to take his hand and go home with him," I said. "Assure her that it's all right to do this. Such a conversation may seem strange to you, but it's a way to help her move gently through the dying process."

Sylvia thanked me, and her eyes told me she was much relieved. I was sure she was seeing the entire experience from a slightly different point of view and had a lot to think about.

"That's Happened to Me!"

It is important to share with the dying some of the phenomena they might experience. I try not to make a big issue of this; rather, I look for opportunities to work it into the conversation as casually as I do the breath prayer. For example, I might say, "By the way, some people who are very ill have out-of-body experiences. If it happens to you, you might feel like you're observing yourself. You could be on the other side of the room, above your bed looking down, or sitting in the chair while staring at yourself in bed. It's a strange sensation, but nothing to be afraid of. Just be attentive to your breath prayer and know that God is there with you."

A great benefit of the breath prayer is that it gives people a sense of security. No matter what they're experiencing, the prayer is a familiar anchor that holds them fast and lessens fears.

Matt was a forty-year-old engineer who had suffered a lingering illness. One day when I brought up the matter of out-of-body experiences, his eyes widened and he blurted, "That's happened to me more than once! Each time I've been scared because I thought I was dying, but along with the fear I had a peaceful feeling, too. The last time it happened, I was across the room looking at myself in bed, and I thought, *That's not even me anymore. I'm more than that body there.* It's strange, but since that time I've had such peace, and I often say to myself. 'I'm more than this sick body.' I haven't wanted to tell Jane [his wife] because I thought it would blow her away. The next time you see her will you mention it, Ron? Then we can talk about it together."

I suggested that I plan my next visit when Jane was there. I would bring out-of-body experiences into the conversation as though I was mentioning the subject for the first time. With me there to back him up, Matt could talk about his experiences in as little or much detail as he felt necessary.

Some people tell me they don't like to ask for pain medication because it makes them hallucinate; they are afraid they might not come out of their hallucination and return to reality. I advise them to take the medication but also to discuss the dosage with their doctor or nurse. Some pain cannot be controlled and as long as theirs can be, they should not suffer needlessly. Here, too, I suggest using the breath prayer. "Begin to say your prayer and keep it going into the hallucination," I tell them. "You'll feel God's presence and be at peace knowing that God will lead you out again."

Called to Our Heavenly Home

Here on earth, we are sojourners in a strange land—sojourners who are called eventually to our heavenly home. Before Jesus died, he said, "I go to prepare a place for you . . . that where I am you may be also" (John 14:2–3). Although we believe this promise, we tend to give little thought to an afterlife until we are confronted with sickness and the possibility of death. Our task as spiritual caregivers is to help people find comfort and hope in what it means to go home to God.

It is not for us here on earth to know what risen life is like. That is something each of us will experience in our own time. In recent years, however, we've had glimpses of what may lie beyond this life. Through advances in emergency medical procedures, many people who would once have been declared dead have been revived. In case after case, those who visited the outer edge of this life tell of great beauty and a feeling of being enveloped in total joy and love.

I don't believe love ever dies. It continues to unite us

even across the divide of death. That's why it came as no surprise when Sylvia told me about her aunt's saying that her dead husband had been to see her. I find it quite natural that loved ones would come to be united with us when it is our time to go to God with whom they already dwell.

God gave us Jesus as the open door for our salvation. I think loved ones who have gone before us may act as bridges across the divide from here to that open door. By making their presence felt, they ease our passage into risen life. Often I find the dying are comforted by the thought that when they pass from this life to the next, they will not be alone. Jesus and their loved ones will be there waiting to welcome them home.

If the dying person to whom I am ministering doesn't bring up the matter of an afterlife, I sometimes take the initiative. "What do you think heaven is like?" is a good conversation opener. It gives people the opportunity to express their ideas and possibly have some of their fears allayed. Once when an old priest friend was dying, we sat talking about what came after death. "I preached a lot about it," he said, "but now I'm not at all sure what heaven will be like. Dying takes a lot more faith than I ever thought it would . . . or maybe I'm just scared that what I preached will turn out to be wrong."

"I know we'll all be surprised," I said, which was the only response that came to mind. It took Karen's death to show me just how happily surprised we will be.

"It's More Than I Ever Expected!"

Jim called and he was sobbing.

"Did Karen die?" I asked.

"N . . . no, but we think it's time. Can you come over?"

I was on my way immediately.

The three of us had often talked about the end time. I told Karen that she would know when it came and that she should tell Jim, or whomever she was with, so that the person could join her in saying her breath prayer. At this point in Karen's illness, she was moving in and out of a state of consciousness where she walked and talked with Jesus. She had also confided that lately she was being visited by her son and first husband who had died years earlier in a car accident; both told her how much Jesus loved her. I had little doubt that Karen's time had come.

The door was ajar when I arrived at the townhouse. After giving a quick rap to signal my arrival, I walked in. Jim and Karen looked up at me with panicked expressions. Karen was in her recliner: no wig, no makeup, nothing artificial. Jim was sitting beside her chair, holding Karen's hand and stroking her arm.

There was a quaver in Jim's voice. "Thanks for coming. We didn't want to bother you, *but we're so scared!*"

"I'm glad you called," I said. "It's a gift to be with you. First let's read some scripture to remind ourselves that we're in God's presence." Then I realized that in the rush I'd left my Bible in the car. "Could I use your Bible?" I asked.

When I made that request, I didn't realize I was going to get a lesson in the amazing things that can happen when we let God take the lead. I had planned to read Psalm 42, which talks about our soul's yearning for God. But when Jim handed me his Bible, it was a New Testament. Feeling flustered, I said, "Don't you have an Old Testament?" He went to look for one, and I realized what a ridiculous request I'd made. I fumbled an apology and said to never mind, this was fine. Opening the New Testament at random, I looked down and saw that I had turned to the Book of Revelation. My heart lurched. I had experienced Revelation as a controversial book and, of all the books in the New Testament, the one from which I did the least teaching and preaching. I scanned the page that was open before me, and my eye fell on the opening verses (1:1–8). I began to read and was astonished at what an excellent choice it was. (Since that day I have often used that particular scripture from Revelation with people who are near death.)

After I finished reading, I prayed for strength and peace. Then I repeated Karen's breath prayer a few times out loud: "*Let* me come to you, O God. Let *me* come to you, O God. Let me *come* to you, O God."

Karen and Jim seemed much more at ease. "Why don't you tell me what happened?" I said.

Karen began haltingly. "When I . . . woke up this morning . . . I had a funny feeling." She paused to take deep breaths. "I remember you said that I'd likely know when it was time. I thought it was and called for Jim."

"And then we both panicked!" Jim said with an abrupt laugh. "It was like the blind leading the blind. So I called you."

"I feel a lot better now," Karen said. "I don't think this is quite it."

"I don't either," I said and then told a story from Eleanor's and my prepared childbirth experience that—in an earlier chapter—I likened to preparing for death. "About four o'clock one morning Eleanor awoke and said, 'I think it's time.' We panicked and then remembered the sheets of instructions we'd been given in class. We read them over together and decided that Eleanor should have a cup of tea and go back to sleep. That's what we both did, and Paul's birth came about a week later."

The story lightened the moment. What Jim and Karen had experienced was the death panic. It is a point at which people feel the end has come and then forget all the preparations they have made for it. That's when it is helpful to have a "coach"—someone to guide them through the panic and over the chasm that separates them from the next life. We visited awhile longer, and before leaving I went over the steps they should take when Karen's time actually came.

A few days later, I was returning from a luncheon meeting when Eleanor met me in the driveway. "Jim just called," she said, "He and Karen are at the hospital." She handed me a slip of paper with their number on it.

I called at once. Jim told me that when Karen got up that morning, the pain was unbearable. "We couldn't get in touch with anyone to give her some shots so we came to the emergency room. They wouldn't do anything unless she was admitted."

The three of us had talked at length about Karen's wanting to die at home while sitting in her recliner and looking out the window at a familiar scene. Now that was impossible. But Karen had the single most important thing she hoped for—Jim was at her side. Her parents had come and gone, the kids were in school, and Jim and Karen decided not to call them. It was just the two of them together as the end approached.

Briefly I recapped what needed to be done: "Remember what we've talked about, Jim. When it's time, Karen will tell you. Although it'll be hard for you, begin to say her breath prayer out loud. Maybe she'll say it with you and maybe not. Whatever, just keep saying it. After saying her prayer for a while, ask her to look for Jesus. When she sees him, tell her to take his hand and go with him. You got all that?"

He said that he did. I asked him to give Karen my love and hung up.

Later that same afternoon, I had a call from Jim: Karen had died.

I met with Jim the following day and asked that he tell me what happened. "It was really something," he said and shook his head, still a bit bewildered. "After you called, Karen whispered, 'What'd he say, Jim?' I repeated what you told me on the phone. No sooner had I finished telling her than she jerked a little and touched her heart. 'Jim,' she said, 'I think this is it."

Tears filmed Jim's eyes as he told how he felt as if the floor had fallen out from under him. Even though I had just talked to him about what to do, his mind went blank. "I just grabbed her hand," he said. "I was desperate! Then—honest to God, Ron,—the strangest thing happened. It was like a power I had never experienced before came over me. Almost without my being aware of it, I was saying, 'Let me come to you, O God. Let me come to you, O God. Look for Jesus, Karen. Do you see him?'

" 'No,' Karen said weakly.

"I kept on saying, 'Let me come to you, O God. Look for Jesus, Karen. Let me come to you, O God. Let me come to you, O God. Do you see Jesus yet, Karen?'

"She just shook her head."

Jim spoke as if every detail of the scene was being replayed in his mind. "Let me come to you, O God. Let me come to you, O God. Do you see Jesus, Karen?"

" 'Y . . . yes,' she said softly. 'Yes.'

" 'Take his hand, Karen,' I kept saying and repeating her prayer. Then Karen turned to me; her eyes were open wide, and there was a kind of astonished look in them. 'Oh, Jim,' she whispered, 'it's more than I ever expected!' And at that moment she died. For a long while I just sat there holding her hand and saying her prayer."

Karen's earthly sojourn was over. She had made the passage to risen life and was not disappointed. Her experience is a reminder to all of us never to hold onto what we think is the wholeness of God. In the end, it is always more than we expect.

11
A Need to Tell the Story

After Karen died, I gave Jim an opening to share with me what her death was like. I knew how important it was for him—as it is for all survivors—to tell what happened in those final moments of a loved one's life. Telling and retelling the story is important for many reasons. It reaffirms the relationship and the love that was shared. Telling the story also serves as a release for the emotions and helps survivors accept the reality of the death.

In cases where survivors can't be present at the time of death, it is critical that they be informed about what occurred in those last minutes and seconds. Unless they have this knowledge, the story they have to tell will always be incomplete. I learned just how much it means to survivors to know the details while on a visit to one of my hospitalized parishioners. I was leaving his room when a nurse grabbed me by the arm. "Please, come quickly, Father," she said and rushed me down the hall. "Mrs. Forth's husband just died, and she's alone in the consultation room."

I didn't know Mrs. Forth. But before I could explain this, the nurse vanished as quickly as she had appeared. I stood for a moment being attentive to my breath prayer and saying a brief prayer for Mrs. Forth as well. Then I opened the door and stepped into the stuffy little consultation room that was crowded with vinyl-and-chrome furniture. Perched on the edge of one of the chairs was a birdlike, silver-haired woman who turned to me with a start.

"The nurse asked me to come and talk to you," I explained after introducing myself as an Episcopal priest. "She said your husband just died." I pulled up a chair so that I was facing Mrs. Forth and extended my hands. She gripped them and began to cry.

"They wouldn't even let me stay in the room with him," she said between sobs. "What will I tell my sons?"

"Are they on the way?"

"They called from the airport. They're renting a car and will be right over," she said, struggling to be composed. "But I won't be able to tell them about their dad's death because I wasn't there! When all the machines started buzzing, the medical people pushed me out of the room. They went to work on Harvey, but it didn't help. He died anyway, and a nurse brought me down here."

Mrs. Forth was suffering the shock that's part of grief. But clearly her biggest concern at the moment was what she would tell her sons.

"Mrs. Forth—" I began.

"Agnes," she requested gently.

"Agnes, I'd like to get the nurse who was with your husband when he died. I think she'll be able to tell you something you can share with your sons."

"*Oh, would you?*" There was a pleading look in her eyes.

I found the nurse who had been in attendance. Her name was Elise, and I quickly explained what I wanted her to do. Her forehead furrowed, and she looked scared. "How can I do that?"

"Just tell her what happened. Use all the clinical information you have, but try to explain it simply. Was he in pain in the end?"

Elise shook her head. "No, he wouldn't have felt pain. In fact, I'm sure he was already dead when the machines went off."

"It's important for Agnes to know that. Would you please tell her?"

"Okay," she agreed apprehensively. "But this is a first for me."

We returned to the consultation room, and I introduced Elise. Agnes hadn't known the nurse's name, but recognized her as someone who had helped care for her husband. Elise sat across from Agnes and gave a clinical explanation of what happened. She concluded by saying, "Your husband's painless death set off the machines."

Agnes nodded knowingly. "I knew he was dead when they went off," she said more to herself than to us.

Elise glanced at me, and I saw tears in her eyes. She had done what needed doing, and I stood up so she would feel free to leave. As Elise rose, she looked to Agnes. "I'm sorry," she whispered. "Very sorry."

Agnes stood and gathered Elise's hands in her own. "Thank you so much for coming. I'm sure this has been difficult for you."

Then Agnes and I were alone again. I asked her if she wanted to repeat what Elise had said to be sure she'd heard it accurately. (I find that in crisis situations people often need help in clarifying what they hear.) Agnes repeated what Elise had told her about the final moments and then went over what she planned to tell her sons. It was a story she would tell and retell many times in the next few days.

We talked a bit longer. Agnes said she was a Presbyterian and had never met an Episcopal priest before. I explained how I happened to come to the consultation room and remarked that God is gracious to have people in the right place at the right time. It seemed natural that we pray together, so we did. I asked especially for peace and strength for the family: for the sons who were expecting to see their father alive for the last time, and for Agnes who would have to tell them about his death. I offered to stay until her sons arrived, but Agnes had gathered her strength and preferred to wait by herself. She had a nostalgic look on her face as she said, "I guess I need a little time alone to think about how wonderful it was being married to that man for forty-seven years."

Someone to Listen

A parishioner of mine woke up one morning and found her husband dead beside her in the bed. Following the funeral, I went to see Janet, and we sat in her living room visiting. Mostly we made small talk about the funeral, and she told me how caring people had been. Then there was a lull in the conversation, and I sensed that the time was right so I said, "Why don't you tell me about it, Janet?"

She began to cry softly, but was composed enough to tell her story down to the smallest detail: what they'd had for dinner that evening, the television shows they had watched, a joke Jack had told her. Then she described the experience of finding Jack dead: how she had called for him to get up several times and he didn't respond (but that was normal), how she got worried when he didn't move at all, how the panic set in, how when the paramedics arrived she knew her husband was already dead. "I guess he died sometime during the night," Janet said, her words now matter-of-fact, "because when I touched him he was already cold."

After Janet had finished with her story, she looked at me and sighed. "Thanks, Ron, that was just what I needed. No one has really wanted to sit and listen to all that. I've tried to tell the story before, but each time I sensed how uneasy it made people—even my own children." She looked down at the wedding band she'd been twisting on her finger. "It's all been building up inside me, and I had to get it out. Now that I have, I think I'm free of it. It's a good feeling."

Listening to the grieving tell their stories is one of the kindest things we can do for them. In most cases, telling the story once is not enough; they need to tell and retell it many times. Doing this is an important part of working through the grief process, a process we facilitate by asking to hear their story and then listening with interest and compassion. A close friend told me that when his mother died, he told a mini-version of his mother's life and death to about fifty people during the viewing at a funeral home. He said that doing so helped him see who his mother really was and how much she meant to him.

Support Systems

Perhaps no one relates to the grieving or listens to their stories with quite as much understanding as someone who has had a similar experience. That is why grief support groups can be so helpful to those who have suffered the loss of a loved one. Many churches already have such groups, and those that don't can provide an important service by starting one.

Grief support groups require little more than meeting space and a trained facilitator who creates an atmosphere of warmth and trust. Beyond that, the grieving help themselves by telling their stories and listening to the stories of others. In the talking and sharing, broken hearts begin to mend.

It is also helpful if pastors have a list of parishioners who can be called upon for one-on-one counseling. No one identifies with a widow's sorrow quite like another widow. Parents who have lost a child feel the heartache of parents in the same situation in ways that others cannot know. Putting such people in contact with one another can be a blessing in life's bleakest moments.

Spiritual caregivers need to know what support services are available in the community as well as the church. In large communities there may be specialized support groups: for example, groups for parents without partners, groups for parents whose infants have died, or groups for survivors whose loved ones have been killed by drunk drivers.

Whenever working with a patient in a hospital setting, it is a good idea to see if there is a pastoral care department, and if there is, what services it provides. An increasing number of hospitals are extending their care to the bereaved. Often that care includes making a chaplain available for the survivors and offering grief support sessions.

As Christians, we believe we live on both sides of physical death. Our task as caregivers is to help the dying move into eternal life and to assist the survivors in finding renewed meaning and purpose.

"What's the Story with These?"

There are many ways to tell the story of a life. A way that was unique in my experience happened the evening after my father-in-law's memorial service. The whole family—wife, children, and grandchildren—was sitting in the living room when someone brought out my father-in-law's jewelry box. In it was an assortment of tie clasps, cuff links, and various other pieces of jewelry. One of the sons suggested that each of us choose something to take as a remembrance. All the family members started looking over the contents. None of the pieces had a great monetary value, so there was no concern that someone was getting something of greater worth than another. As each person made a choice, my mother-in-law recalled a story about the item. "That was an anniversary gift." "Those he got on our trip to Ireland."

I selected a pair of cuff links with blue stones. "What's the story with these?" I asked.

Laughing, she said, "He got those at St. Vincent de Paul

Second Hand Store. We had cleaned out our closets and taken a load of clothing there. He spotted those cuff links, and I think he paid twenty-five cents for them."

We all had a good laugh over that. Now whenever I wear them I am reminded of my father-in-law's generosity and how he could be as comfortable in a twenty-five-cent pair of cuff links as he was in much more expensive jewelry.

Stories at Funerals

When I preach at funerals, I encourage people to take time to write down a story or remembrance they have of the deceased. Frequently people are present who have meaningful recollections that the immediate family knows nothing about. Working such remembrances into the eulogy helps personalize a funeral and make it memorable for everyone. Often such recollections include touches of humor.

In order to gather these stories, small cards (three-by-five or four-by-six) can be made available at the funeral home. On them print, "One remembrance I have of (*name of deceased*) that I would like to share with the family is: _____." Afterward the cards can be given to the family. The stories on them will likely be read, remembered, and treasured for years to come.

Another way to share stories is to invite those attending the funeral to stand up and tell something about what the deceased meant to them. This, too, is an effective way to make the funeral a loving celebration that leaves family and friends with warm memories.

At Karen's funeral, Jim requested that their pastor talk about the breath prayer and how meaningful it had been for Karen and the family. He then asked the congregation to sit in silence for a few moments and say to themselves, "Let me come to you, O God. Let me come to you, O God."

The prayer was a way to tell the story of Karen's acceptance of her death and of the faith that sustained her.

Telling the Story and Moving On

A few years ago I had a seriously ill parisioner named Joe. About once a week I would stop by his house to see him and his wife, Helen. As Joe's condition worsened, my visits became more frequent until finally I was stopping to see him every day. After Joe died, I was still attentive to the family. They needed to talk about his life and his death and have someone listen. I went less and less frequently as time passed, and one day I realized I hadn't made a visit in over two weeks. When I did stop by, Helen said, "I wondered if I had to get sick to see you more often."

The hint of sarcasm in Helen's words made me realize that the visits to Joe were visits to her as well. First I would talk to Joe—usually until he dozed off—and then Helen and I would sit in the kitchen and visit. Now I understood that she still needed that contact, and I assured her I would stop by more regularly.

Helen had continued to use her husband's breath prayer: "Let me feel your peace, O God." It made her feel close to him and kept his memory from fading. I know it is helpful for survivors to use the breath prayer of the deceased for a while, but there comes a time when they have to adjust to life as it is—to life without the one they mourn. About eight months after Joe's death I was making one of my periodic visits to Helen, and she told me about a new career she was starting. The moment seemed right to ask, "If the Lord were right here in front of you saying, 'Helen, what do you want?' what would you say?"

"I guess I'd say, 'Let me see the way, O Lord,' " she replied.

"Then I think it's time for you to have your own breath prayer. In the past, Joe's prayer was good for all of you. But now you're moving on. That doesn't mean you'll ever forget Joe, or that what you shared means any less to you. It's just that you've grieved deeply and well. Because of that, you've found the strength to fashion a life for yourself."

Helen nodded her agreement, but admitted that it was a scary venture.

"Remember," I said, "you'll have your breath prayer to help see you through."

"Let me see the way, O Lord," she mused. "That really seems to suit me now, doesn't it?"

I agreed that it did indeed.

12
Developing Your Own Approach

Jesus said, "I was hungry and you gave me food, I was thirsty and you gave me drink . . . I was sick and you visited me." This statement perplexed his listeners, and they asked when they had performed these kind actions. His reply: "As you did it to one of the least of these my brethren, you did it to me" (Matt. 25:35–40).

The expression "my brethren" refers to all people in need. The sick and dying are truly in need, and often what they most hunger for is not food and drink but spiritual sustenance. They yearn to feel God's loving presence and to be assured that beyond this life of pain and anxiety lies something more promising. They need to hear from a person of faith that God's promise will be fulfilled and that they will "walk in newness of life" (Rom. 6:4).

Those of us who feel called to be spiritual caregivers need to care about the suffering of others, need to share our faith through prayer, need to be people of hope that we might give hope. But for hope to be helpful, it must be honest and realistic.

Sometimes we have such an urge to comfort that we raise false hopes. This is most likely to happen with inexperienced caregivers. Such was the case with Bill, a young seminarian who was spending time with me so he could get some training. I took him along one day when I went to visit Elma, an eighty-one-year-old widow whose husband had been dead for over twenty years. Her five children lived in various parts of the country and rarely came to see her. They seldom wrote either. On my first visit to Elma, she shared a letter from her daughter and showed me some pictures. Six months later she was still sharing the same letter and showing me the same pictures.

On the day Bill came with me, Elma was more talkative than usual and lamented the fact that her children didn't write more often. Bill picked up on her disappointment and said, "This is a very busy time of the year. I suspect you'll hear from them soon. You know they love you."

Elma gave Bill a sad, dismissing look that said he really didn't understand at all.

Bill was acting out of a desire to say something comforting, but his well-intentioned comment caused him to lose credibility. How much better it would have been had he said nothing and simply nodded sympathetically.

No Two Heartaches the Same

A familiar old spiritual goes, "Nobody knows the trouble I seen, nobody knows my sorrow." What wisdom those plaintive lines contain! My experiences have taught me that there is no way I can completely share in the sorrow of others. Grief is unique, and each individual suffers in a personal way. Yet people try to give comfort by saying, "I know *exactly* how you feel." This kind of comment is an affront. We can never get completely into someone else's mind and heart; we can never know precisely how another person feels. We can, however, try to find something from our own experience that shows we have some understanding of the person's situation.

To someone with a terminal illness, we might say, "When I'm sick, I feel as though my body has betrayed me."

To a survivor who has lost a loved one, "When my mother died, I found out how painful a loss can be."

To a shut-in, "There are times when I'm alone and find myself wishing I had something useful to do."

Such statements convey warmth and interest without presuming to know what is going on in another person's innermost self.

Learning and Growing

In stressful situations—such as entering a hospital room to visit a dying person for the first time—we may jump in with inappropriate comments because we can't handle our own feelings or are uncomfortable letting others express theirs.

Think how you felt the last time someone began crying in your presence. Were you ready to encourage the tears as a necessary expression of emotion? Did you believe the tears needed to fall before that person could accept the situation and perhaps gain new insight? Or did the tears make you feel uncomfortable? Did you think it was your responsibility to get the person to stop crying and cheer up? If such was the case, the crying may have stopped, but emotions that needed the release of tears went unexpressed.

Although I've been ministering to shut-ins and the dying for many years, the work never becomes routine or easy. Each encounter is a learning experience. Sometimes I still come away from a visit wishing I'd done this or hadn't done that, said this or hadn't said that. But I believe we learn as much from what we do ineptly as from what we do with skill and grace.

Reviewing the Approach

There is no neatly prescribed way to work with those in physical and emotional pain. Though each case is different, the breath prayer is a unifying element in our work. Let's review the major ideas we've covered.

Discover your own breath prayer. We like to share what we believe in and what works for us. If you haven't discovered your own prayer and found that it opens your heart to where God is leading you, you won't be enthusiastic about sharing it with others.

Introduce the breath prayer in a casual manner. Most people who are seriously ill or dying don't want to be "taught" anything, but they long for something concrete they can do that will help them help themselves. Once you have developed rapport with a person, casually mention the breath prayer as something you and many other people have found useful. Help those who are interested discover their own prayer.

Leave a card with the person's breath prayer printed on it. In many cases the elderly are forgetful and the ill are on medications that fog the memory. When the breath prayer is written down and placed where it will be seen often, it is repeated and remembered. Over time, saying the prayer becomes as natural as breathing.

Take the risk. Whenever you put forth a new or different way of doing something, you take a risk. You risk being thought foolish, and you risk rejection. But I've come in contact with only a few people who haven't been receptive to hearing about the breath prayer. In a small number of cases, people have discovered their prayer and then not found it useful. Perhaps they didn't persevere long enough to realize its benefits. For me, the breath prayer has been so personally rewarding and spiritually enriching that I find sharing it with others to be a risk well worth taking.

Develop your own style of relating. In recounting my experiences, I have not intended to lay out a blueprint or give a formula for you to follow. Rather, I wanted to show that I have developed my style of relating just as you will develop yours. You have a special way of caring and nurturing. God doesn't want you to be anybody but yourself—the best self you are capable of being. A rabbi named Zusya was saying this when he wrote, "In the coming world they will not ask me: 'Why were you not Moses?' They will ask me: 'Why were you not Zusya?' "

Give the gift of touch. Although some people don't like to be touched, they are the exception rather than the rule. My experience indicates—and studies show—that when you touch people, they believe you care about them. As you develop rapport with those you visit, let your compassion and instincts guide you in the matter of how and when to touch. Remember that those of us who go to others with the intention of praying have an advantage. Most people will take our hands when we reach out and ask, "Can we pray together?"

Give the booklets. The time you can devote to any individual or family is limited. In addition, people in stressful situations don't always fully comprehend what you say to them. So it's helpful to have printed material that you can leave behind. These three booklets offer you the opportunity to speak to patients and their families when you can't be there in person.

When I'm Alone: Thoughts and Prayers That Comfort. This booklet is meant to be given to the patient at the time the breath prayer is explained. It reviews the procedure for discovering one's own breath prayer and includes consoling thoughts and additional prayers for the long, lonely hours when there is no human voice to give comfort and reassurance.

Near Life's End: What Family and Friends Can Do. This booklet is to be given to those who are concerned about the practical, everyday matters they must face as they watch someone they love move toward death. It includes prayers and quotations meant to uplift and encourage caregivers.

A Time to Mourn: Recovering from the Death of a Loved One. This booklet is to be given to family and friends upon the death of the patient. It is written to help survivors accept their sorrow and move through it.

Commit yourself. When you take on the work of ministering to shut-ins, the sick, and the dying, you become intimately involved in their lives. They may be people you hadn't known previously and might never have known were it not for their infirmity or illness. You enter their lives at a time of need, and they count on you to be there for them. You become their friend and trusted confidant, often hearing intimate personal stories, outpourings of anguish, and admissions of guilt. They are saying they trust you, and you show yourself to be worthy of that trust by being trustworthy. Your friendship and commitment nurture their spirit and help them find the strength to face loneliness, pain, and death.

The work of a spiritual caregiver is intense and often emotionally draining. But remember, you are not alone. God has promised to be with you always. Let your breath prayer be a reminder that in whatever circumstance you find yourself, God is there to guide, to strengthen, and to sustain you.

As Christians, we understand that death is both an ending and a beginning. In some mysterious way, when we witness a death we are also witnessing the birth of a new life. One of the prophets of our faith poetically expressed the idea of death's overcoming darkness when he wrote, "At evening time there shall be light" (Zech. 14:7). We who are privileged to work with the sick and the dying can help make the ending of life what a glorious sunset is to a meaningful day: A time of tranquillity and peace. A time of looking back at what has been, and a time of looking forward to a new day in the light of risen life.

Into the Light is part of a total program created by Ron DelBene to help people share more deeply with those who are sick or dying. Should you wish to purchase additional copies of this book or copies of the booklets listed below (and described on pp. 140-41), please order them through you local bookstore or write to: Upper Room Books, Book Order Dept., P.O. Box 189, Nashville, TN 37202-9929.

When I'm Alone: Thoughts and Prayers That Comfort

Near Life's End: What Family and Friends Can Do

A Time to Mourn: Recovering from the Death of a Loved One

Ron DelBene holds a master's degree in theology from Marquette University and has done additional post-graduate work in education, psychology, and counseling. He has been an assistant professor of theology, director of a campus ministry center, and National Consultant in Religion for an education division of CBS. Since 1963, Ron has been conducting programs in the area of religion—integrating educational, psychological, and therapeutic approaches to growth and development with religious experiences.

Grounded in his parish ministry experience, Ron presently leads retreats and conferences on prayer and spiritual direction. He is an Advisory Board Member and Faculty of the National Academy for Spiritual Formation sponsored by the United Methodist Church. He has worked with various denominational judicatories in retreat and spiritual formation work, as well as Cursillo, Walk to Emmaus, and Kairos (a prison ministry).

Ron is an Episcopal priest and the Missioner for Spiritual Development for the Diocese of Alabama. With his wife, Eleanor, he directs The Hermitage, a place for people to enter into solitude and prayer under their direction. He has published numerous articles and is also author of *The Breath of Life, Hunger of the Heart,* and *Alone with God.*

Ron and Eleanor and their two children, Paul and Anne, live in Trussville, Alabama.